# STARTUP OPPORTUNITIES
## KNOW WHEN TO QUIT YOUR DAY JOB

by Sean Wise & Brad Feld

FG PRESS | BOULDER, COLORADO

*Startup Opportunities: Know When to Quit Your Day Job*

©2015 Sean Wise & Brad Feld

EDITOR | Dave Heal

CREATIVE DIRECTOR | Kevin Barrett Kane

FG PRESS, *Publishers*

PHYSICAL | ISBN 978-1-941018-00-2 | $24.95 in the USA, $29.95 in Canada

DIGITAL | ISBN 978-1-941018-22-4 | $9.95 in the USA

TO AMY AND MARISA,
*Our wives, who are by far the best*
*opportunities we have ever invested in.*

# TABLE OF CONTENTS

# PREFACE

ENTREPRENEURS OFTEN DREAM of that magical moment in the creative process when they will have a flash of clarity about how to solve a problem or make a product in an innovative way. And they often have an interesting story to tell about this moment, with the origin stories of some successful companies becoming legend. Yet this moment of clarity often obscures the massive amount of work required to go from an idea to a real startup. From the outside looking in, a great company appeared out of nowhere. But the entrepreneur knows differently and remembers what had to happen to get from the idea to even the most embryonic startup.

As investors we hear a simple question from entrepreneurs multiple times a day: "What do you think of my idea?" Sometimes the idea is well formed; often it is vague. Some have already been prototyped, others are just a few sentences in an email. Some have been deeply researched by an entrepreneur with deep domain knowledge, others are something completely new and different that the entrepreneur is exploring.

While it is easy to have an idea, it is incredibly hard to translate that idea into a successful business. The startup phase of a company requires a wide variety of activities to go from idea to successful startup. In the past few years, many books have been written about this process. Some foundational ones include *The Lean Startup* by Eric Ries, *The Startup Owner's Manual* by Steve Blank, and *Disciplined Entrepreneurship* by Bill Aulet.

However, we continue to hear some version of the same question over and over from aspiring entrepreneurs. "Is my idea any good?" Sometimes it's phrased as, "How do I know if my idea is good?" or "When I have an idea, how do I know if it's good?" Often, this morphs into "I have the following three ideas. Which is the best one?"

These entrepreneurs aren't ready to stop what they are doing and dive all the way in to chase their new idea. Many have full-time jobs and are trying to figure out how this entrepreneurship thing works. Some are playing around with multiple ideas at the same time and trying to pick one. Others are stuck in the ideation phase, coming up with ideas and looking for external validation, but are unwilling to commit to working on one yet.

Ultimately, they are asking some form of this question: "Will there be enough demand for this product that people will use it and pay for it?" Even after being pointed at books and approaches like *The Lean Startup*, they still have questions about whether their idea is any good.

It's not a simple question to answer. Most successful companies go down a long and winding journey to find the answer. It used to be that you wrote a comprehensive and tightly structured business plan that evaluated all aspects of the potential business. This document often took hundreds of hours to write and tried to set up the theoretical case for the business without actually testing anything.

While business planning isn't obsolete, the business plan is. It has been replaced by concepts such as the Business Model Canvas, Business Model Generation, Lean Startup, Lean Launchpad, and

Disciplined Entrepreneurship, which all use a structured, experimental approach with quantitative feedback loops from potential users, customers, and partners to evolve the idea to a foundation upon which a startup can be built. Different approaches to an idea or a business can be tested and iterated upon quickly using these methodologies.

But that still leaves us with the questions: "Is the idea any good?" and "Should I pursue this idea?"

We believe it is possible to get to a better starting point if you spend some time in the *opportunity evaluation* phase. Before you even begin testing the idea and building on it, there are some fundamental questions you can ask. Through our work at Techstars, *Dragons' Den*, and as early stage investors, we have found ourselves asking entrepreneurs a set of questions over and over again. While many of our conversations were short, and detailed answers often weren't forthcoming, we found that even the simple act of asking the questions often helped the entrepreneur improve the idea.

It is not good enough that you think your idea is a good idea. Others need to agree with you to such a degree that they'd be willing to join you on your journey, either as partners, employees, investors, advisors, or customers. However, many entrepreneurs are afraid to share their idea with others for fear that it might be stolen. But as you'll see in a moment, ideas need oxygen. In addition to engaging supporters and getting feedback, opening ideas up and sharing them with trusted advisors at the very beginning can help evolve these ideas into something that you can really build.

Our goal with this book isn't to replace methodologies like Lean Startup. Instead, we want to complement them by giving you a context and a set of tools to help you evaluate your idea before you start putting any meaningful energy into it. Think of this exercise as the precursor to the Lean Startup or the Lean LaunchPad approaches. We want this to be the book you read before diving into one of these methodologies, especially if you are a first time entrepreneur.

The audience for this book isn't just investors or current entrepreneurs, but a much larger class of readers—those who have yet to quit their jobs and take the leap into entrepreneurship.

# TRUST ME, YOUR IDEA IS WORTHLESS

## by Tim Ferriss[1]

EARTH-SHATTERING AND WORLD-CHANGING ideas are a dime a dozen. In fact, that's being too generous.

I've had hundreds of would-be entrepreneurs contact me with great news: They have the next big thing, but they can't risk telling me (or anyone else) about it until I sign some form of idea insurance, usually a nondisclosure agreement (NDA). Like every other sensible investor on the planet, I decline the request to sign the NDA, forgoing the idea, often to the shock, awe, and dismay of the stunned entrepreneur.

Why do I avoid this conversation? Because entrepreneurs who behave this way clearly overvalue ideas and therefore, almost by definition, undervalue execution. Brainstorming is a risk-free, carefree activity. Entrepreneurship in the literal sense of "undertaking" is not. Strap on your seat belt if you're signing up for a startup. It's a high-velocity experience.

If you have a brilliant idea, it's safe to assume that a few very smart people are working on the same thing, or working on a different approach to solving the same problem. Just look at the number of different travel apps on your iPhone or the number of diet and exercise sites on the Web for an example of this.

Overvaluing the idea is a red flag, particularly in the absence of tangible progress. Sure, I miss out on investing in some truly great ideas with this attitude, but that's okay with me: I don't invest in ideas. Nor does Warren Buffett. I'll lose less money than those who do. I can largely control my downside by investing in good people who, even if they fail this go-round, will learn from mistakes and have other fundable ideas (ideas I'll likely have access to as an early supporter). I do not have this advantage when investing in ideas.

One popular startup dictum worth remembering is "One can steal ideas, but no one can steal execution or passion." Put in another light: there is no market for ideas. Think about it for a second: have you tried selling an idea lately? Where would you go to sell it? Who would buy it? When there is no market, it is usually a very sure sign that there is no value.

Almost anyone can (and has!) come up with a great idea, but only a skilled entrepreneur can execute it. Skilled in this case doesn't mean experienced; it means flexible and action-oriented, someone who recognizes that mistakes can often be corrected, but time lost postponing a decision is lost forever. Ideas, however necessary, are not sufficient. They are just an entry ticket to play the game.

Don't shelter and protect your startup concept like it's a nest egg. If it's truly your only viable idea, you won't have the creativity to adapt when needed (and it will be needed often) in negotiation or responding to competitors and customers. In this case, it's better to call it quits before you start.

Your idea is probably being worked on by people just as smart as you are.

Focus on where most people balk and delay: exposing it to the real world. If you're cut out for the ride, this is also where all the rewards and excitement live, right alongside the 800-pound gorillas and cliffside paths. That's the fun of it.

David didn't beat Goliath with a whiteboard. Go get amongst it, and prepare to bob and weave.

1.  Brad Feld and David Cohen, *Do More Faster: TechStars Lessons to Accelerate Your Startup*, (Hoboken: Wiley, 2010), p. 3–5

# WHAT IS A STARTUP?

THE WORD *"STARTUP"* HAS BECOME an increasing part of the popular lexicon in the past few years. While it has been around for a while, it has recently become ubiquitous for those talking about entrepreneurship and new company creation. But not all new companies are startups.

There is a big difference between two types of entrepreneurial endeavors: (1) *local businesses*, also called SMEs (small- and medium-sized enterprises) or lifestyle business, and (2) *high growth companies*, often referred to as startups or *gazelles*,[1] a term first used by David Birch in 1979 and refined in 1994 to refer to companies with at least $1 million of revenue that were at least doubling in size every four years.

Local businesses are what they sound like. These are the businesses that you find in your city whose customers are close to the business, such as the corner grocery, local bookstore, non-chain restaurant, or locally owned gas station. Occasionally these local businesses start to expand and turn into multi-geography businesses, resulting in a large enterprise, but many are local businesses for their duration.

In contrast, high growth companies rarely have a local focus. While they are often started in one location and at inception usually only have a few people involved, the founders of these companies have aspirations to grow very quickly, independent of geographic boundaries. Their customers are all over the world and, regardless of whether the company ever expands geographically, the business is rarely constrained by geography.

In the United States, until recently, all startups were referred to as small businesses. This is an historical artifact of the US Small Business Administration, commonly referred to as the "SBA." Until 2010, the US government didn't differentiate between types of entrepreneurial businesses. As a result, the SBA was helpful to some companies but useless to many others, especially the high growth ones. Government at all levels (federal, state, and local) didn't really understand the potential impact of startups as a separate class of company, and so all small businesses were lumped together.

In 2010, President Obama announced Startup America[2] and as a result the word startup catapulted to the forefront of everyone's minds. Through the support of the Case Foundation and the Kauffman Foundation, the Startup America Partnership was launched. This was a private partnership that executed a three-year plan, chaired by Steve Case (the founder of AOL) and led by Scott Case (unrelated to Steve), to define, support, and spread the message of startups throughout the United States.

Today, a startup is recognized as something distinct from a small business. For the definition of startup, we turn to the czar of customer development and grandfather of the Lean Startup movement, Steve Blank, who has coined what we think is the best definition for the term.

According to Steve Blank, "A startup is a temporary organization formed to search for a repeatable and scalable business model."[3]

Let's break down his definition and explore the different parts:

- *a temporary organization*: A startup does not last as a startup. It either goes out of business or succeeds in finding a solution that customers are willing to pay for.
- *to search*: The goal of a startup is to explore, test, and validate an unmet need. This definition recognizes that the startup lifecycle is finite.
- *repeatable and scalable business model*: Initially, all startups are based on assumptions, with the goal of iterating until the assumptions have been validated. Once the business model has been proven and the startup is self-sustainable, it is no longer a startup.

As Steve has stated, a startup is not a small version of some future big company. It is a series of experiments in the search of a scalable business.

## HOW TO USE THIS BOOK

Our goal with this book is to help you figure out in advance which ideas are worth experimenting with. While this book is intended to be read from beginning to end, we have organized it so that you can read each section independently. We want to provide you with a structure to evaluate the idea you have in a formal and comprehensive way while allowing you to quickly think about the key issues that will come up.

We aren't trying to create a new methodology for starting a company, nor are we trying to replace approaches like Lean Startup. Instead, we are taking a step back and engaging earlier in the process. This book is intended to be read before you read *The Lean Startup* or engage in a Lean LaunchPad process. We'll provide plenty of context around different approaches and resources for getting your business off the ground, but our primary focus is in helping you with the pre-startup, or the *opportunity evaluation* phase, when you are still deciding whether or not to put energy into the startup.

In addition to our perspectives, we've included a number of examples from entrepreneurs and the investors who funded them at very early stages. Many of the examples are of companies that have grown substantially. By going back to near their inception, you can get a sense of how and why the entrepreneur and the investor decided to pursue the opportunity. Other sidebars include expert analysis from practitioners or academics of some of the more important elements in the opportunity evaluation process.

Our primary professional focus is in investing in high growth startups. Brad's experience, through Techstars and Foundry Group, is primarily in high tech companies. Sean's experience, through *Dragons' Den* (Canada's version of *Shark Tank*) and his own investing, is primarily consumer products. In an effort to make this book applicable for anyone interested in starting a company, we've used examples from each of these domains.

### WHO THIS BOOK IS FOR

We wrote this book with first-time entrepreneurs in mind. However, we have received feedback from experienced entrepreneurs that the ideas in this book have been helpful to them in thinking through their next opportunity.

As entrepreneurship engages a wider range of younger people in our society, we are finding a dramatic increase in entrepreneurship from high school and college students. This book is directly aimed at them and is intended to be used as a part of an entrepreneurship curriculum.

This book is for educators, particularly those teaching entrepreneurship and opportunity recognition and evaluation courses. If you are a teacher whose students often ask, "How do I know if my idea is worth pursuing?" then this book is for you.

This book is also for friends and family who support the entrepreneur on their complicated and challenging journey. If you are an entrepreneur, you can use it as a source of dialogue with your spouse, your siblings, your parents, and your children.[4]

This book is for fans of *Dragons' Den* and *Shark Tank*. If you ever wondered how the judges choose which companies to fund, this book is for you.

This book is also for investors, especially angel and early stage investors, as they try to better understand a new business. In the same way that the entrepreneur can use this book to help shape their opportunity, an investor can use the same concepts to help evaluate an opportunity.

Most of all, the book is for all those who have a passion of entrepreneurship. Those who know that only the very best opportunities deserve their blood, sweat, and tears. Ideas may be worthless, but your time, energy, and focus are not. Friends only let friends work on great opportunities.

1.  John Case, "The Gazelle Theory," May 15, 2001, *Inc.*, http://www.inc.com/magazine/20010515/22613.html

2.  The White House's *Startup America* homepage, http://www.whitehouse.gov/economy/business/startup-america

3.  Steve Blank, "What's A Startup? First Principles," January 25, 2010, *Steve Blank's blog*, http://steveblank.com/2010/01/25/whats-a-startup-first-principles/

4.  Don't forget your pets, especially if you have a rubber duck. For more perspective on the value of talking out loud to yourself, see http://en.wikipedia.org/wiki/Rubber_duck_debugging

# CHAPTER 1

# OPPORTUNITIES

AT SOME POINT IN YOUR LIFE you've had an entrepreneurial epiphany. You suddenly came up with an idea that you couldn't stop thinking about. You might have believed it was an idea that could change the world and bring you fame and fortune. It might be something that you wanted to create to solve a problem you had. Or it could have just been something you were completely fascinated by and obsessed with.

Throughout history, whenever there is a problem or an unmet need, humans have tried to create something to provide a solution. The academic literature talks about these unmet needs as being the result of "suboptimal solutions," a status quo that leaves the user or customer unsatisfied. The telegraph was invented to address the fact that the postal service was a suboptimal solution for rapid communication and addressed the unmet need of instant communication over large distances. Airplanes provided a solution to suboptimal long voyages by ship. Facebook aggregated and improved upon a number of different suboptimal solutions for sharing information with your friends and family.

## THE FOUR CRITERIA FOR AN OPPORTUNITY

All opportunities start with an idea. While ideas are at the heart of all opportunities, for an idea to be seen as an opportunity, it must be actionable (i.e., an idea that can't be executed isn't an opportunity) and have the following characteristics:[1]

1. *The idea is durable*: It is not a fad and will last long enough to allow for monetization.
2. *The idea is timely*: The market is ready to buy the solution.
3. *The idea is attractive*: The potential rewards and returns on investment far exceed the foreseeable costs and resources to create the product.
4. *The idea adds value*: It must lead to a product or service that creates or adds value for its buyer or end user.

Sean has spent years listening to pitches from entrepreneurs seeking investment on the business reality show *Dragons' Den*, the Canadian version of *Shark Tank*. Throughout this book we'll include short examples from *Dragons' Den* or *Shark Tank* to illustrate our points. We will start with DJ R Dub,[2] an entrepreneur with an idea that missed on all four of these characteristics. DJ R Dub came on *Shark Tank* to raise capital for his "love song dedication show." It didn't go well. The investors declined to fund this entrepreneur on the grounds that the idea was not:

*Durable*: The audience/market for radio talk shows is shrinking.

*Timely*: The golden age of radio is long over, having been cannibalized by iTunes, online streaming services, and other music apps.

*Attractive*: Running ads against content requires a huge audience and this audience has migrated away from the radio.

*Value*: The founder was focused on a younger audience, yet this demographic gets its music from places other than the radio.

## WHAT IS OPPORTUNITY EVALUATION?

While opportunities are often obvious in hindsight, it's hard to evaluate the opportunity when the idea first comes up. The moment the idea occurs to an entrepreneur, it's rarely obvious that the opportunity will be a significant one, often because the market is unknown, the technology is non-existent, or the idea is so radical compared to the currently available solutions.

Since our time, energy, bandwidth, and capital are scarce, it is useful to differentiate good from bad opportunities regardless of the role you play in the entrepreneurial ecosystem.

- Entrepreneurs have to choose which opportunity to pursue.
- Employees need to decide which companies to join.
- Investors have to choose which opportunities to fund.
- Customers decide which products to buy.
- Governments and NGOs need to decide which opportunities are worthy of public resources.

Opportunity evaluation is the systematic, objective assessment of the potential of an opportunity[3] and we refer to the unit of measure as the *quantum of return.*

The quantum of return can be the amount of money you think you can make from an opportunity. Investors call this *return on investment,* or *ROI.* For example, the ROI of a one-year, 3% government bond is 3%. If you bought $1,000 of bonds, you would receive $1,030 at the end of the year for an ROI of $30, or 3%. Not very inspiring, but that's because it's a low risk investment. Another quantum of return is based on the amount of time you spend on the opportunity. This is commonly referred to as *opportunity cost of time* or *return on invested time (ROIT).*[4] Humans have an average life expectancy of about 25,000 days. How you spend each day—which is to say, how you "invest your time"—should factor into the attractiveness of pursuing a specific opportunity.

The concept of return on invested time applies to entrepreneurs as well as employees of a startup. As your startup begins to grow, you will need to convince people to join your team instead of being part of a company pursuing a different opportunity. If these prospective employees are going to spend years working for you, they need to believe that they will get a better return on invested time. If your software developer passes up working at Google for $90,000 a year, then her time at your startup must generate more wealth than she is passing up. Her decision must also take probability into account. Working at Google is nearly guaranteed to pay her $90,000. To lure her to your startup, the wealth potential must be greater after accounting for the risk that the startup will fail. In mathematical terms:

$$(10\% \ chance \ of \ success) \ x \ (potential \ value \ of \ equity)$$
$$>$$
$$(100\%) \ x \ (\$90,000) \ x \ 3 \ years$$

While it is difficult to determine the probability of success, one's qualitative reaction to the notion of expected ROI and ROIT impacts the decision to pursue an opportunity. In hindsight, ROI and ROIT are important quantitative measures, enabling you to look back and measure how things went. After all, a billion dollar idea that fails isn't as valuable as a million dollar idea that succeeds.

## WHAT IS THE COST OF POOR OPPORTUNITY EVALUATION?

According to the Global Entrepreneurship Monitor in 2013,[5] some 465 million people between the ages of 18 and 64 around the world were actively engaged in early stage entrepreneurial activities. Consider how many of these people are pursuing poorly thought out opportunities, resulting in lost time, effort, and money.

There is an endless stream of opportunities around us each day. Some are good and some are not. Many people fixate on the opportunities missed. Over the years, we've continually heard statements like "XYZ is a great business. I had the idea for XYZ years earlier." These statements are often followed by the speaker rambling on about how wealthy she would be if she had pursued the idea for XYZ.

But the value of the opportunity is often only apparent in hindsight. While the entrepreneur may come up with the idea, if no action is taken then the statement "I had the idea for XYZ years earlier" is irrelevant. Ideas without execution are worth very little.

For example, Mark Zuckerberg was not the first person to explore or build a social networking product and company. But, once it became a success, many people wanted to take credit for coming up with the idea, and, by extension, the business. The famous quote from the movie *The Social Network*—where Mark Zuckerberg says to the Winkelvoss brothers during a deposition, "If you guys were the inventors of Facebook, you'd have invented Facebook"—rings true.

The cost of what could have been created is small when compared to the resources squandered on bad ideas. If an entrepreneur spends all his time, energy, social capital, bandwidth, and money on an idea that turns out to be a poor opportunity, in addition to being out all the time, energy, social capital, bandwidth, and money invested in the poor opportunity, the entrepreneur has a large *opportunity cost*.

Opportunity cost represents "the cost of an alternative that must be forgone in order to pursue a certain action and the benefits you could have received by taking an alternative action."[6] For example, if an executive decides to go back to school to obtain her MBA, in addition to direct costs (tuition, school books, and bus fare), she will have opportunity costs (salary not earned while in school and work promotions not pursued). In order to understand the true cost of the MBA, one has to account for both direct costs and opportunity costs.

While poor opportunity evaluation has direct costs, the opportunity costs are often even more substantial. For every bad idea that moves forward, the resources and direct costs are unavailable for the better ones. Venture capitalists (VCs) invested $29.4 billion in 3,995 deals in 2013, an increase of 7% in dollars and a 4% increase in deals over the prior year. It is commonly asserted that only 1% of companies that pitch VCs get funded. If 3,995 companies got funded, there were hundreds of thousands of companies that pitched VCs that didn't get funding. What's the disconnect? One of the explanations is poor opportunity evaluation by entrepreneurs.

Poor opportunity evaluation isn't limited to VC-backed companies. Of all the businesses that are started each year, less than half will survive past the five-year mark and a third will be dead within 24 months.[7] Poor opportunity evaluation isn't the sole cause of these failures, but it is a major contributor.

FOUNDER'S PERSPECTIVE
## SENDGRID, by Isaac Saldana (Co-founder)

As I've gotten older, I have come to realize what matters most to me when making decisions about how to spend my time. I've found there are four aspects to consider, relative to the situation, that make my decision-making easier. These aspects are resources, relationships, knowledge, and happiness.

Resources include getting minerals in a video game, more vacation in a job, oxygen in a workout, or shares in a company. Relationships refer to a network in business, great chemistry and productivity with co-workers, or a great and loving relationship with your wife and kids. Knowledge is powerful because it can't be taken away until death and it can be transferred to the people that I care about. Finally, happiness, according to the documentary *Happy* by Roko Belic, can be achieved by being healthy, experiencing something new, spending time with friends and family, doing some type of play or game, being thankful for what you have, and understanding that you make a difference. If I find a good balance among these four aspects I can easily move forward with a decision.

Initially, I didn't know SendGrid was a good business opportunity. SendGrid is an email infrastructure service that helps companies deliver transactional email. The data available before I started SendGrid was limited and did not provide good insight into the size of the market or any sign of demand. Email marketing companies existed, but they did not address developers, the main target audience for SendGrid.

I had other potential ideas I could work on that seemed interesting. Unfortunately, the company where I was working at the time was experiencing email deliverability problems and I could not put this problem away. Since I was not an expert on this issue, the more time I worked on it the more interested I became in actually solving it. Experiencing new problems, learning new protocols and technologies, and solving them with new approaches kept me going, kept me happy, and kept me learning. Eventually I realized there was the potential for innovation in the email space since I had to solve most of the problems I was experiencing. In this sense, I would be scratching my own itch.

But I still needed validation that an email infrastructure solution could be a real business. Armed with an initial solution, I asked around several Internet forums related to web hosting if anyone was experiencing email deliverability issues and was interested in a solution. To my surprise, a web hosting company replied that they were interested in offering my solution to all of their customers. I then approached the two smartest engineers I knew, pitched the idea of an email infrastructure company, and they joined. I was no longer on my own exploring this opportunity. I now had a team.

A few months later, we applied to a startup accelerator called Techstars and got accepted. It is harder to get accepted to Techstars than Harvard, so this provided validation from the seasoned entrepreneurs, companies, mentors, and investors who are part of the Techstars network. Soon after we went through Techstars, we raised nearly a million dollars from Highway 12 Ventures. We later got acquisition offers but chose instead to grow our business and went on to raise over $20 million dollars from Foundry Group and Bessemer Ventures. At this point, we have over 200 employees and millions of dollars in monthly recurring revenue.

I believe there is still much to do in the email space, so SendGrid has a great opportunity in front of it. Understand what matters to you, how you stay excited, and how you can make a difference. Startup opportunities are all around us. Which one will you pick?

## SENDGRID, by Mark Solon (Techstars, Highway 12 Ventures)

I first met Isaac, Tim, and Jose, the founders of SendGrid, during the second week of the 2009 Boulder Techstars class. I spent 30 minutes with each of the ten Techstars teams that day and left with a strong positive feeling about SendGrid and its three founders. It was obvious to me in that brief meeting that Isaac was obsessed with solving the problem of large volume, transactional email deliverability because it had caused him a great deal of frustration in his role at a previous company. I left that first meeting with a feeling that Isaac was on a mission to solve this problem and nothing was going to stop him. Four years later, what stands out in my mind about that meeting was that Isaac and his team were able to clearly and succinctly articulate the pain point in the market they were going after.

When I returned to Techstars a month later and met with them again, it was apparent that they were making terrific progress. SendGrid was signing up developers as customers on a regular basis at a low enough price point that they weren't forced to jump through hoops for approval. By keeping the price low (less than $100 per month), they made it easy for their customers to simply put the service on their credit cards. They were keen on removing any obstacles for customer adoption and knew they'd have opportunity later to charge for more features and benefits once they had a loyal customer base.

The other thing I observed was that all the other Techstars teams were enamored with Isaac. Many of them went to him for technical help and they all had great things to say about both the team and the solution. In addition, most of the other teams were already customers of SendGrid. What great validation!

With a month left in the program, I started talking to Isaac on a regular basis. With each conversation, I knew in my gut that he was a very special entrepreneur. Despite his soft-spoken nature, I came to believe that inside him burned an incredibly determined entrepreneur. I arrived at Techstars Demo Day with a term sheet to lead the SendGrid seed round.

SendGrid checked three important boxes (team, market, and idea) for me to lead their seed round. Team trumps everything for me at the seed stage. From my perspective, Isaac, Tim, and Jose were serious and credible founders with strong technical chops. Next, they were going after a real pain point in a large and growing market. Finally, their solution worked and wasn't cost prohibitive.

I feel lucky that I've been a small part of SendGrid since its inception. Today, SendGrid has over 100,000 customers, delivers over half a billion emails each day and is regarded as one of the most important cloud infrastructure companies in the world. As an investor, opportunities to invest in companies like SendGrid don't come around every day and they're not necessarily easy to spot at the seed stage. While SendGrid had many early signals that it had the potential to become a very large and important company, it was only through the hard work and great early execution by Isaac, Tim, and Jose that gave the company the chance to be what it is today.

## EXECUTION TRUMPS OPPORTUNITY

When Tim Ferriss says "Trust Me, Your Idea Is Worthless," he means it. Mary Kay Ash, the founder of Mary Kay Cosmetics, famously stated, "Ideas are a dime a dozen. People who implement them are priceless." In the absence of execution, your idea doesn't go anywhere. Opportunity evaluation helps improve your starting conditions, but you still have to execute.

### EXECUTION IS WHAT REALLY MATTERS
(Professor Steven A. Gedeon, PhD, MBA, PEng)

Entrepreneurship is a fundamental spark of human initiative that enables us to act and shape the world around us. It is about belief in yourself, your ability to create positive change, and your capacity to inspire others to join you in your great adventure. It is about starting with nothing but your own mind and creating dramatic new products and services that didn't previously exist. Entrepreneurship is the most empowering, creative, freedom-loving power in the world.

Entrepreneurship is more than a business discipline. It is a core way of seeing, thinking, and acting that is relevant to all disciplines, faculties, and people. Entrepreneurs don't just see the world as it is, they see it as it can or ought to be and then they make their vision into reality. While entrepreneurs are inventors, planners, thinkers, dreamers, and opportunity spotters, none of these attributes matter if they are not also doers.

Entrepreneurship is about creating value that must be brought forth into existence before it can be exchanged, sold, or used. Even something as abstract as "intellectual property" must be crystallized into a concrete form such as a written document (patent), creative work of art (copyright), or logo (trademark).

Execution is everything. An idea or a business plan has no value on its own. Investors say that they invest in an A team with a B plan over a B team with an A plan. Why? Because business plans are always wrong. Despite all the great analysis and planning, things will go wrong. Sales will take longer, product development will evolve the product into something different than originally envisioned, founders might leave, or a competitor could enter the arena. Often, several of these happen at the same time.

Stability for a new company is like stability on a motorcycle. When the motorcycle is stationary or moving slowly, it easily falls over, seems to weigh a ton, and is difficult to get back up again. Yet at high speeds its spinning wheels act as gyroscopes to keep you upright. Barriers that seemed insurmountable when you were pushing the bike up a hill become slight bumps in the road when you are travelling fast.

The more quickly you act, the more stable your company becomes and the greater your chance of success. Perfectionists make lousy entrepreneurs. Don't waste time on the perfect business plan—it's probably wrong anyway. Don't delay speaking to customers, making sales, or launching your product as you wait for the perfect moment. Get out there—now!

Initiative, passion, and execution are the only things that you, the entrepreneur, really have under your direct control. With that in mind, here are a few specific principles of entrepreneurial execution:

*Be an Evangelist*: Get out there and talk to everyone who shows interest in your business, including potential customers, suppliers, employees, investors, friends, and peers. Don't keep your idea a secret. Don't disclose your secret sauce, but if your idea or ability to execute is so weak that others can steal it, then let them take it and instead move on to something that you can execute better than anyone else.

*Be a Skeptic*: Don't just talk. You have two ears and one mouth—use them in that ratio and listen! Ask hard questions and don't let people get away with telling you what they think you want to hear. Don't just hear the nice things people say. Go deeper and keep asking questions until you find something they don't like or understand. You need to tell people great things about your company, but don't let that blind you to the possibility that your company is not as great as it could be.

*Be an Examiner*: Set, measure, and track goals. There are more things in a business to keep track of than any single human being can accomplish without a serious project management mindset. Accordingly, you need to find a way to track the goals that really matter and focus your team on achieving them. You need to find a way to translate long-term goals into daily actions. These goals have been referred to as things like key success factors, milestones, OKRs,[8] and targets. You need to make sure everyone on your team is singing from the same songbook.

*Tie Rewards to Performance*: Align everyone in your organization toward key metrics. Don't just pay people for showing up and looking busy.

*Tie Organizational Structure to Strategy*: Figure out what each of your key strategic activities are and put an executive in charge of each one so these activities don't fall through the cracks. Don't just have an organizational structure that gives each founder a VP title with no corresponding key activity. There is no need to use traditional titles like VP Tech or VP Marketing simply due to a lack of imagination or ego inflation on the part of co-founders or early employees. Make sure your executives know which aspects of the business they are responsible for.

*Question your Assumptions and Adapt*: Most successful companies make numerous course corrections early in their lives. Since the chance your original business plan is correct is very low, you should assume from the beginning that you will make major changes to your product, team, and market. As you get out there and present your products and services, you should be learning and changing.

*Be a Role Model*: You, the entrepreneur, breathe life into the company you create. You instill your values, passion, and work ethic into the company, which creates a company culture through your habits and character. If you show up late, so will your employees. If you can't make and keep commitments, neither will your company. In the early stages of a company, you are the living personification of the character that your company will become. Be a role model for your team in order to lead a great company.

## RISK, UNCERTAINTY, AND AMBIGUITY

Entrepreneurs face many challenges when starting up a new company. Often these challenges are grouped together and collectively referred to as *risk*, which oversimplifies the situation and often results in a narrow view of what is going on. We like to separate the notion of risk into three different categories: *risk*, *uncertainty*, and *ambiguity*.

Risk occurs when action or inaction may lead to loss, dealing with a future state that may be negative and often can be quantified. In contrast, uncertainty deals with future states that cannot be known and cannot be predicted or quantified. Finally, ambiguity implies knowledge that is unclear. We separate these into three constructs because risks can be mitigated through action, uncertainty is resolved through the passage of time, and ambiguity can be addressed by additional investigation.

While risk takes on many forms, focusing on a few helps clarify what risk really is, and how to mitigate it. Nobel Prize recipient Herbert Simon suggested the term "bounded rationality" to describe a more realistic conception of human problem-solving ability. Since humans have finite brainpower and limited time to apply this brainpower, they cannot be expected to solve all difficult problems optimally. Finding the optimal solution often takes more time and resources than would be, well, optimal. You don't drive for 100 miles to get $0.01 off a gallon of gas. You don't visit ten supermarkets to find the lowest price for every item on your grocery list. Tradeoffs have to be made. As a result, we adopt benchmarks or rules of thumb to help us bound the number of ideas we have to explore when making a decision.

Cole Egger and James McDonald mitigated market risk with their Sweet Ballz[9] dessert by working with national retailer 7-Eleven to generate $700,000 in sales in the first 90 days. In doing so they got firsthand market data and validation of their product through sales to end customers. Nathan Jones and Erick Jansen used the crowdfunding site Kickstarter to mitigate market risk for their product, The Freeloader,[10] an ultra-sleek child carrier that has an integrated frame and a fold-down seat that can hold up to 80 pounds. These two firefighters sold $40,000 in product on Kickstarter before they had even produced it.

Another risk is management risk, which asks the question "Is this the best team?" If you are a solo founder, you are the team! While there are cases of solo founders being successful, the odds are against you. Our experience with Techstars has shown that the ideal team size is two to four founders, with at least half of them being focused on the product. If you are a solo founder, you can mitigate this risk by finding a co-founder.

In contrast to risk, uncertainty is much harder to address. Typically, uncertainty is the absence of specific data or support for a particular concept that can only be addressed by the passage of time. Rather than ignore uncertainty, there is significant value in articulating it during the opportunity evaluation phase. Clearly stating what the uncertainty is and trying to nail down how long it might take to resolve will help clarify things. If the uncertainty is unbounded and will last forever, that's a real problem. If the uncertainty will be resolved after six months of a particular activity, that's manageable.

Finally, ambiguity can be addressed continually throughout the life of the company. It's particularly useful to focus on this during the opportunity evaluation stage, as clarifying issues and situations that are ambiguous and can be debated helps bring clarity to the opportunity.

## THE ISSUE OF BIAS

Opportunity evaluation is a highly subjective process. Whether you are an entrepreneur or investor, you will bring your own history, experience, knowledge, and perspective to the process of evaluating a particular opportunity. We refer to this as *bias*. While bias is helpful, it can also be dangerous since it often impacts evaluations significantly and creates blind spots that can be difficult to mitigate. It's important to know and understand your own biases in the context of an opportunity.

## KILLER BIAS: PSYCHOLOGICAL TRAPS THAT CATCH ENTREPRENEURS AND INVESTORS
### (Professor Dave Valliere, MEng MBA PhD PEng)

Every day, everywhere around the world, opportunities are being evaluated and significant resource commitments are being made. Which startups to fund? Which founders to back? These are questions with enormous social and economic consequences. Look around and you'll see these killer biases happening everywhere, including in yourself. If you know them in advance, you can avoid the killer bias trap.

There are all kinds of people who need to know how to spot a great business idea. Some are entrepreneurs trying to decide whether this is the opportunity into which they should put their heart and soul. Some are investors trying to discover the one that will yield returns big enough to offset the other failed investments they've made. Some are potential employees, suppliers, business partners, or intermediaries. Each has a different perspective and different objective for the opportunity evaluation process. But all operate with the same flawed human mind, trying to assess the idea and potentially falling prey to the same common psychological biases—the kinds of traps that catch everyone unless we are fully aware of them and take steps to avoid them. The following are four of the most pervasive psychological biases that often trick both entrepreneurs and their investors into making bad decisions that can kill new ventures and wipe out investments.

*Confirmation bias* or *willful blindness* arises whenever we have formed a strongly held opinion or view about something, particularly when we have made a big effort to gather and analyze a lot of information before arriving at our opinion. There are two dangerous effects that may result from confirmation bias. First, one can become attuned and receptive to information that appears to support their opinions. People tend to notice every newspaper article that can be interpreted to support their belief. Investors who have fallen prey to confirmation bias tend to view and accept as true every occurrence in the world that can possibly be seen as an example of the phenomenon in which they believe.

The second dangerous effect of confirmation bias is that one can become blind to information that appears to refute their opinion. Reviewers suffering from confirmation bias often cease to look for information that might contradict their pre-formed opinion. Furthermore, if the world shoves the conflicting information into their faces they find some way to rationalize it or deny it. They say "yeah, but…" and then find some trivial difference that allows them to dismiss the contradictory evidence as an irrelevant special case rather than change their opinions, since that would mean admitting being wrong in the first place. It can suddenly seem like confirming cases and examples are everywhere around us, and it can appear that no counter evidence exists. This is an illusion—the rates of occurrence and nonoccurrence have not changed. It is only our awareness and perception that have changed.

Because of this, entrepreneurs and investors should always attempt to remain flexible and open to the possibility that their opinions and assumptions may turn out to be false. Opportunity evaluators should attempt to always remain humble and receptive to the reality that the marketplace will try to teach them. They should make sure their assumptions are open to being proved wrong.

But it's often not enough if entrepreneurs don't also take active measures to counteract confirmation bias. Investors face the same challenges around confirmation bias and are generally more difficult to coach, especially once they've formed an opinion about whether a market space is hot. Both entrepreneurs and investors need to take deliberate actions to keep confirmation bias in check, such as intentionally seeking out contradictory information or contrarian opinions from experts. The real test of whether you have a good business idea is not your ability to find information that says "yes," but your inability to find information that says "no."

*To avoid confirmation bias, spend your time trying to find information that refutes your beliefs instead of more information that supports them.*

The next killer bias is *over-confidence*, which is having a belief in one's abilities that is greater than the objective facts warrant. While it is good to have entrepreneurs who are highly talented and who know it (confidence), entrepreneurs who are unable to recognize the limits of their remarkable talent (over-confidence) can cause problems. This is a particularly hard bias to detect in oneself, since people who are over-confident in their abilities are usually also over-confident in their self-awareness and ability to correct for their own biases. Over-confidence is actually an umbrella term that encompasses a group of related biases, including the *planning fallacy* or the "90/90 rule" (i.e., the first 90% of a project takes the first 90% of the budget, and the final 10% of the project takes the second 90% of the budget), and *personal attribution error* (i.e., if things go right it's because I'm so smart and skilled, but if things go wrong it's because someone else screwed up.) Both are examples of having unreasonably high beliefs in oneself.

Psychometric tests of entrepreneurs and investors repeatedly show some amazingly high levels of over-confidence. This is a real cause for worry. These individuals are highly confident and are perfectly right to feel that way since they are highly skilled and capable. In fact, one might argue that confidence is a necessary trait for both entrepreneurs and investors. But, while their abilities might well be 50% better than the average person, they tend to think and act as if their abilities were 500% better. For entrepreneurs, this means they often think they can accomplish much more than they can, and that their chances of succeeding in a risky venture are much better than they actually are. The same phenomenon holds for investors, who will be over-confident in their abilities to pick winners and add value to their investments. There's a real lesson in the observation that most VC funds have a hit ratio of only 1 in 10 investments becoming successful. But most VC investors are unable to learn from it because they are caught in their own over-confidence.

*To avoid over-confidence bias, make your decisions based on objective data about what you actually have achieved in the past, not what you subjectively think you should be able to do in the future.*

The third killer bias is *availability bias*, which is the mistaken belief that situations that are easy for an individual to imagine must be very common out in the world (or the converse—that if you've never personally seen a black swan[11] they must not exist.) While this is seductive reasoning, it is false logic and it can be extremely dangerous to generalize too widely. With proper perspective we can see that our own experience, while a deep and vivid source of insight, is still just a dataset with a sample size of one, which is hardly enough to use as the foundation for an entire business strategy. Statisticians will remind us that any sample with fewer than 40 responses will fail to meet even the most basic assumptions of statistical significance. We should guard against this bias by reminding ourselves regularly that the plural of anecdote is not data.

Entrepreneurs who are caught by this bias often exhibit *the market is me behavior*—they believe that if they like the proposed new product, then thousands of other people are going to like it also. This is a weird conclusion, especially since we celebrate entrepreneurs for being so unlike other people, for thinking and seeing so differently than others, and for being willing to act where other people would not. Therefore, they are often not suitable to use as benchmarks for the marketplace.[12]

The exact same problem occurs on the investor side of the table. In their case it often sounds something like, "I heard that BigVCFund got a 10x exit in the cloud computing space, so I'm going to invest in the next cloud deal that crosses my desk."

*To avoid availability bias, keep reminding yourself that your experience is unique and that there is no reason to think that it corresponds to what real market data would say about the average person.*

The final bias to be wary of is a phenomenon known as *prospect* theory, which explains three interrelated biases. First, people give too much emotional weight to small chances, thinking that a 1% chance is much better than no chance at all and that a 99% chance is much worse than a sure thing. The strength of this belief can be witnessed at any lottery ticket kiosk. Secondly, people treat chances of winning something much differently than they treat the chances of avoiding the loss of something. For example, we usually have to offer the chance of winning at least $250 to entice people to accept a chance of losing $100. Thirdly, people judge these wins and losses not in absolute terms, but relative to where they expected to be or where they told other people that they'd be, which is known as their "anchor point." These biases combine to create a two-sided irrational phenomenon that catches many people off balance. On the one hand, if we are winning (or even if we are losing, but not as badly as we expected to lose) we tend to become overly conservative and reluctant to take sensible or attractive gambles. We try to lock in our wins, thinking that a bird in the hand is worth two in the bush. On the other hand, if we are losing (or even if we are winning, but not as grandly as we told everyone we would) we tend to become reckless risk-takers who throw Hail Mary passes in the slim hope that we can catch up to where we think we ought to be.

This phenomenon is the mechanism that drives *escalating commitment*, which is when one throws good money after bad in the hopes that the original losses can still be somehow salvaged. This is based on the stubborn human refusal to recognize that *sunk costs* are always irrelevant when making a decision in the present moment. An investor who has watched the value of his investment fall in a clearly doomed startup company will still be strongly biased to participate in any subsequent round of funding in a futile attempt to keep the company alive for a bit longer to avoid having to accept that the first round money is irretrievably lost.

Prospect theory warns opportunity evaluators that they cannot trust their gut instincts when assessing probabilities of success and that their perceptions will be strongly skewed by recent history. It says that they must ignore the emotional perception that losses hurt more than wins elate and that they must be particularly careful when announcing targets lest they become anchor points that will force them into irrational escalating commitments. Investors may love entrepreneurs who set "kickass" targets and, blinded by their over-confidence, loudly proclaim that these *Big Hairy Audacious Goals (BHAGs)*[13] will be achieved or exceeded. Such acts come with huge risks of becoming trapped in biases that will drive bad decisions and destroy value.

*To avoid escalating commitment biases arising from prospect theory, use objective calculations to determine the expected value of uncertain choices, and be very careful about the public commitments you make.*

1. Jeffrey A. Timmons and Stephen Spinelli, *New Venture Creation: Entrepreneurship for the 21ˢᵗ Century*, (McGraw Hill International, 2010).
2. *Shark Tank*: Season 5, Episode 4.
3. J. Michael Haynie, Dean A. Shepherd, and Jeffrey S. McMullen, "An Opportunity for Me? The Role of Resources in Opportunity Evaluation Decisions," *Journal of Management Studies*, 46(3) (2009): 337-361.
4. Razvi Doomun and Nevin Vunka Jungum, "Business process modelling, simulation and reengineering: call centres," *Business Process Management Journal*, 14(6) (2008): 838-848.
5. GEM 2013 Global Report, January 20, 2014, http://www.gemconsortium. org/docs/3106/gem-2013-global-report
6. MoneyTree Report by PricewaterhouseCoopers LLP and the National Venture Capital Association, based on data from Thomson Reuters, Q4 2013/Full-year 2013, http://www.pwc.com/en_US/us/technology/assets/ pwc-moneytree-q4-and-full-year-2013-summary-report.pdf
7. SBA Office of Advocacy, Frequently Asked Questions, https://www.sba. gov/sites/default/files/FAQ_Sept_2012.pdf
8. OKRs are "objectives and key results." For a great video from Rick Klau at Google Ventures on how Google sets goals, see https://www.gv.com/lib/ how-google-sets-goals-objectives-and-key-results-okrs
9. *Shark Tank*: Season 5, Episode 1.
10. *Shark Tank*: Season 5, Episode 3.
11. If you are unfamiliar with black swans, we encourage you to read Nassim Nicholas Taleb's book *The Black Swan: The Impact of the Highly Probable.*
12. There is a big exception, which we've called "scratching your own itch." The story of the founding of SendGrid from earlier in the chapter is a great example of this.
13. Jim Collins, *Built to Last: Successful Habits of Visionary Companies* (New York: HarperCollins, 2002), Ch. 5.

# CHAPTER 2

# APPROACHES TO OPPORTUNITY EVALUATION

THERE ARE ALMOST AS MANY APPROACHES to opportunity evaluation as there are opportunities. However, we think that most approaches fall into one of two categories: (1) a stage–gate process or (2) a feedback loop-based approach involving agile decision-making.

A stage-gate process has a series of stages—typically discovery, scoping, building the business case, development, testing, and launch. Between each stage is a "gate," which prompts a review and a decision of whether to go to the next stage, do more evaluation, or kill the project.

The feedback loop process follows a build, measure, and learn approach that is based on the belief that you can only get the information you need by beginning to build what you think your customers want.

The stage-gate process often produces a business plan, which asks the question "*Is this opportunity worth pursuing?*" while the feedback loop process produces something in a form similar to a business model canvas and asks the question "*What assumptions would have to be true for this to be an opportunity worth pursuing?*"

## WHERE DOES OPPORTUNITY EVALUATION FIT INTO THE OVERALL STARTUP PROCESS?

Most attempts to model the entrepreneurial process note opportunity evaluation as a key stage in the creation of a new venture. The cliché "look before you leap" applies, and evaluating an opportunity before investing time, energy, and money is the best way to do that.

The Duke Center for Entrepreneurship and Innovation suggests that the entrepreneurial process can be broken into distinct phases, namely:

1.  Idea Generation
2.  Opportunity Evaluation
3.  Planning
4.  Resource Acquisition
5.  Launch
6.  Growth

# DUKE CENTER ENTREPRENEURIAL PROCESS MODEL

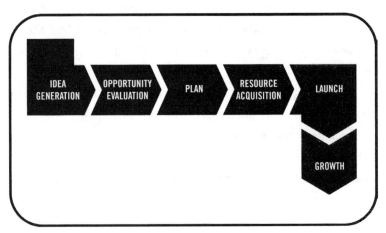

Barringer and Gresock (2008) describe the application of the Stage–Gate model to opportunity evaluation as follows:

# BARRINGER AND GRESOCK (2008) STAGE-GATE MODEL[1]

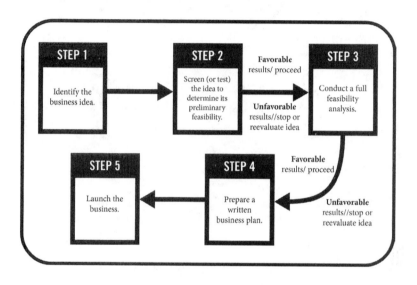

Today, many feel that new venture creation follows a much less direct and much more iterative journey such as the one outlined in Eric Ries's Lean Startup model (next page).

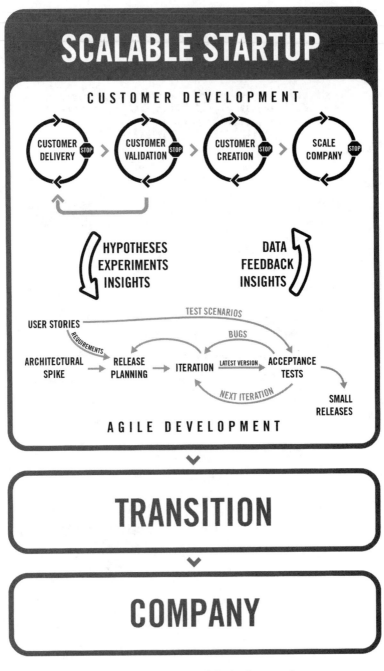

Adapted from an Eric Ries slide that borrows from
J. Donovan Wells's *Extreme Programming*[2]

The idea of a startup evolving as the result of many repetitive iterations of customer development suggests anything but a linear path to success. Thomas Edison is famous for saying, "I have not failed. I have just found 10,000 ways that don't work." It's no surprise that the phrase "fail faster" is firmly embedded in today's entrepreneurial vernacular.

The evolution of Steve Blank's Customer Development and Alex Osterwalder's Business Model Generation to Eric Ries's *Lean Startup* continues as more people study, experiment, dissect, and iterate on the startup process. Recently Bill Aulet, head of the Martin Trust Center for MIT Entrepreneurship, published *Disciplined Entrepreneurship*, a new approach building on what has come before, but incorporating many lessons learned from companies created and launched at MIT.

Opportunity evaluation can be used in advance of each of these approaches to get more clarity on what to work on, before the iterative loop begins. Opportunity evaluation is meant to be a nimble starting point to create focus to apply to a Lean Startup, Lean LaunchPad, or Disciplined Entrepreneurship process.

## OVERVIEW OF BUSINESS MODEL GENERATION

Osterwalder, with his concept of Business Model Generation, suggests that all business opportunities start by examining the basic fundamentals of any business model. By defining and exploring nine core elements of a business model, you challenge and investigate the underpinnings of a potential opportunity, converting the elements into testable hypotheses. The nine components of the Business Model Canvas are:

1. Value Proposition
2. Customer Relationships
3. Channels

4. Customer Segments
5. Key Partners
6. Key Resources
7. Key Activities
8. Revenue Streams
9. Cost Structure

The template for the business model canvas is as follows:

# OSTERWALDER (2010) BUSINESS MODEL CANVAS

| KEY PARTNERS | KEY ACTIVITIES | VALUE PROPOSITIONS | CUSTOMER RELATIONSHIPS | CUSTOMER SEGMENTS |
|---|---|---|---|---|
| | KEY RESOURCES | | CHANNELS | |
| COST STRUCTURE | | REVENUE STREAMS | | |

By addressing each of the building blocks above, you can begin to identify the assumptions on which your opportunity rests. After all, if you can't access the customer segments efficiently, you may have an opportunity with great potential but with no ability to proceed. By adopting the use of the business model canvas, you will explore the obstacles ahead while always keeping the following Machiavelli "quote" in mind:

*Entrepreneurs are simply those who understand that there is little difference between obstacle and opportunity and are able to turn both to their advantage.*[3]

## OVERVIEW OF CUSTOMER DEVELOPMENT AND LEAN STARTUP

Sean started working with startups in 1997 while he was with Ernst & Young. His job was to facilitate the success of high-growth ventures. Fresh out of law school, and with only his own entrepreneurial experience to rely upon, he immediately began looking for a Rosetta Stone of startups, a magical key that would help him understand why some startups fail while others succeed. Fifteen years later, he found it.

During the summer of 2012, Sean studied under Stanford Professor Steve Blank. The class was on how to teach the Lean LaunchPad approach to students, and it changed how Sean thought about startups. Steve's basic tenets can be summarized as:

- No business plan survives first contact with customers.
- Get out of the building to find answers.
- Launch early, launch often.

Steve asserted that spending months writing a business plan and then raising funds in secret to build a product in stealth mode was fundamentally wrong. After his own experience raising a lot of money only to flame out after failing to launch a product that customers bought, Steve tells founders that they should work with customers to refine a crude product into a great product. He favors a more dynamic process, one where founders launch a minimal prototype that does only the one thing that customers need and then tests this product with actual customers.

Judging success on customer feedback allows market demand to validate the founders' efforts. After all, if the pain being solved is so large that customers will accept a less than perfect solution, founders could spend their time improving the product, not searching for a market. This idea of *customer development* was a radical departure from previous approaches to starting a business. No more spending two years and two million dollars on a fully robust solution only to find out that customers don't care.

In Steve's class, Sean learned about Steve's prodigy, Eric Ries, who in 2008 had coined the term Lean Startup.[4] Ries integrated Steve's customer development concept with theories and processes from agile development and lean manufacturing. Like Steve, Eric believed in collaborative development. To Eric, *lean* means:

- *Low Burn*: Only spend money on the basics. Save the bells and whistles for later.
- *Customer Feedback*: Don't fall in love with your hypothesis and assumptions. Don't push products; allow customers to pull them.
- *Rapid Prototyping*: Build something quickly, which is referred to as a *minimum viable product* (*MVP*), and then test it with customers. Use what you learn to make changes to the prototype and repeat until your crappy prototype becomes an awesome solution.

Ries dubbed this idea *ferocious customer-centric rapid iteration* and it has gone on to become the foundation of the Lean Startup movement.

## OVERVIEW OF THE DISCIPLINED ENTREPRENEUR

After having been a multiple-time entrepreneur who got better each time, Bill Aulet returned to his alma mater, MIT, to teach students what he wished he had learned 20 years earlier when he began his first startup. He wanted to create a rigorous yet practical approach where he assembled all the best and proven tools to increase an entrepreneur's odds of success, and then provide a roadmap for when and how to apply the tools. He codified what he had learned the hard way in his experiences while also working with academics to ensure proper perspective and rigor.

The result is an iterative 24-step process called "Disciplined Entrepreneurship" that helps students progress from "I have an idea/technology/passion" to "I have a product that people are paying me money for." He recently codified this approach in his new book, *Disciplined Entrepreneurship: 24 Steps to a Successful Startup*.

The 24 steps in the framework can be categorized into six themes:

- Who is your customer?
- What can you do for your customer?
- How does your customer acquire your product?
- How do you make money from your product?
- How do you design and build your product?
- How do you scale your business?

The process is highly iterative and each step is designed so that as you learn more, you will find reason to go back and revise your work in earlier steps. The framework is designed to help entrepreneurs, particularly first-time entrepreneurs, understand where to start and how to move forward to create a product that customers will want and will result in an economically sustainable new venture.

Disciplined Entrepreneurship can be used for all kinds of new ventures—hardware, software, services, and consumer products regardless of whether a for-profit or mission-driven model will be used. Startups such as Okta, Lark Technologies, Locu, FINsix, FastCap Systems, WeCyclers, Shop Soko, and Essmart have benefited from this approach.

Disciplined Entrepreneurship has proven valuable because it does not seek to reinvent entrepreneurship, but rather to integrate many of the proven techniques that are discussed in individual books and resources.

## A MODERN VERSION OF THE SCIENTIFIC METHOD

If you think back to high school science, a lot of this may feel like an entrepreneurial version of the scientific method. According to the Oxford English Dictionary, the *scientific method* is defined as:

> *A method or procedure that has characterized natural science since the 17th century, consisting in systematic observation, measurement, and experiment, and the formulation, testing, and modification of hypotheses.*

The key words in the above definition are: systematic, measurement, and experiment. Under this discipline, an entrepreneur should no longer rely solely on her gut but should instead systematically observe, test, and measure her assumptions before proceeding, The results of these efforts will help provide the raw material for responses to typical investor questions such as:

- Why offer this solution?
- How do you know your customers want this?
- How did you determine price?

Answer these questions with facts derived from direct customer testing and you stand on solid ground. Answer these questions with anything else and you are on shaky ground. The Lean Startup and the Customer Development cycle that underlies your exploration provides a systematic, testable, and measurable technique to apply the scientific method to startup development and growth.

To use this approach, entrepreneurs should first produce a Lean Canvas (this is a tool explored in more detail later) filled with *testable hypotheses*, which are falsifiable claims (claims that can be disproved) that can be objectively tested using the scientific method.[5] Such a hypothesis must be stated in a way that makes it easy to show when it is wrong. The following are some examples:

- I believe that users want to send messages from point A to point B faster than courier, fax, or phone. (email)
- I believe, globally, more people want to access general knowledge than can afford the Encyclopedia Britannica. (Wikipedia)
- I believe that people want to send and receive email while away from their desk. (Blackberry)
- I believe teenagers want to send messages that expire and can't be recorded for later use. (Snapchat)

All of the examples above:

- are assumptions underlying a business model
- are written down
- can be proven wrong
- can be actionable
- can be tested with customers using a minimal viable product (MVP)

Eric Ries and Sarah Dillard summarized this on the Harvard Business School blog.[6]

*Firms that follow a hypothesis-driven approach to evaluating entrepreneurial opportunity are called "lean startups."*

*Entrepreneurs in these startups translate their vision into falsifiable business model hypotheses, then test the hypotheses using a series of "minimum viable products," each of which represents the smallest set of features/activities needed to rigorously validate a concept. Based on test feedback, entrepreneurs must then decide whether to persevere with their business model, "pivot" by changing some model elements, or abandon the startup.*

One of our favorite stories on the topic of testable hypotheses comes from serial entrepreneur Dan Martell, CEO and founder of Clarity.FM. Dan explained that he tested his initial web-based MVP by including a "Buy Now" button. His hypothesis was that if the service he offered was valuable, users would want to buy it. The "Buy Now" button didn't actually work, but instead led the user to a simple landing page that said thank you and acknowledged them for the input. After the "Buy Now" button was clicked thousands of times, Dan knew he had a solution customers wanted. With this proof of concept in hand, Dan was confident in building out the rest of his solution.[7]

FOUNDER'S PERSPECTIVE
### UBOOLY, by Carly Gloge (Founder)

Walking down the toy aisle we were amazed at how toys have regressed since our childhood and how the industry is now completely based on brand affiliation rather than value. We started Ubooly with a goal that seemed simple enough—to make a magical stuffed animal powered by your iPhone. Our toy would automatically update with new content over Wi-Fi, which would enable us to pump new value into the product each month.

Like a lot of startups we charged ahead, naïve to the challenges of distribution and adapting to consumer behavior—possibly the biggest barriers between a great product and success.

Our first test was on Kickstarter, an important step in determining whether there was an audience that cared about what we were building. The initial burst of users that we gained through this campaign provided the critical insight needed to steer us towards a larger opportunity.

I think it is typical for startups to begin with the premise of "This would be awesome!" only to find out later that no one is actively searching for that awesome thing, if for no other reason that it simply hasn't ever existed. The initial product we built was simply a better toy, and we were lucky that our community guided us down a rabbit hole filled with more meaningful aspirations. We received requests from parents asking if Ubooly could teach their kid a new language and discovered that the toy was being used as a therapy tool for kids with autism.

Our customers told us of an itch that could not be scratched by mainstream toys. We realized that a smart toy wasn't the draw. Parents want smart kids. It seems obvious, but we had completely missed the mark in the beginning. This new wisdom has changed the way we think about our business. Knowing the levers that parents respond to when they are thinking about their kids gives us a path to become a billion dollar brand. Our mission is no longer to deliver a toy that talks and listens, but to help grow kids into smarter, more creative, and overall better human beings.

This big opportunity also comes with a big goal. In order to produce a toy that delivers on all of those promises, we'll need kids to play with our toys for a very long time. This is why our number one goal is retention. After a year of focusing on keeping kids engaged each day, we now have more than seven times the retention of other toys. A sticky product that delivers on a need that users are searching against—this is a product that can grow organically. It may seem like a slow path to entrepreneurs in the enterprise space, but when competing against consumer products that are powered by astronomically high marketing dollars, growth through your customers can be an amazing foothold. While the big boys are pumping millions into advertising budgets to sell kids on their next toy, the Ubooly community grows, and continues to engage with and share a product that they trust.

This also means that when we release new products and content, we don't need to pay to re-acquire our own customers. The average American kid receives 70 new toys each year (a big opportunity), but Mattel spends $700M annually on marketing to sell just ten of those toys. To play in this space we can't compete on spend. We've come to realize that real opportunity comes from striking a nerve, not shiny new products. While shiny new products can get you press and possibly funding, soon those folks will move on to the next shiny product. In our case, real opportunity comes from delivering access to education in a format that kids can't put down—concrete value in the eyes of our customers.

## UBOOLY, by Stephanie Palmeri (SoftTech VC)

To call my investment in Ubooly, a talking stuffed creature, unusual for a VC seems an understatement. At my VC firm, SoftTech VC, we categorize Ubooly within the "new areas" section of our fund given its unique and potentially disruptive nature. But when you look beneath Ubooly's cute, fuzzy exterior, you find an edutainment company that lies at the intersection of several key investment themes for my firm—including mobility, education, and the Internet of Things—with a strong founding team and a differentiated go-to-market strategy.

Focusing on the market first, we have witnessed a proliferation of smart devices being used at home by children as young as toddlers. When we invested in Ubooly, 30% of children played with smartphones, and that number continues to climb. These devices have become a conduit for education and learning. Finally, Ubooly capitalizes on the usage of smart devices to power traditionally inanimate objects.

The most critical element to the success of a startup is its founders: the folks who transform a vision into a company. We believed Ubooly's founding team was uniquely primed to capitalize on this edutainment opportunity. Carly Gloge's experience building startup brands, Isaac Squire's technical expertise, and their combined track record building successful mobile apps through their first business together were strong signals.

Ubooly's Kickstarter pre-orders also provided a strong indicator of the market opportunity. While founders increasingly leverage crowdfunding and pre-order platforms today, Carly and Isaac were early movers on this front. For the Ubooly team, Kickstarter backers helped steer the company towards its emphasis on education. For investors, the Kickstarter campaign not only demonstrated early customer and retailer demand, but also gave us early an indication that international demand was extremely high.

It's not hard to stand out when you pitch a talking orange stuffed animal to investors, but beyond its cute-factor, Ubooly offered a unique value proposition to its customer (parents) and its consumer (children). It combined entertainment value for children (a toy children are excited to play with) with education value for parents (my child is learning as they play). Plenty of gaming apps entertain but leave children sedentary and parents feeling guilty for screen time. Conversely, retention is a major issue for many education-focused apps—they just aren't fun. Ubooly struck a distinctive balance between a toy children find engaging and a companion parents trust to make their children smarter.

Ubooly's distribution and monetization models also made the company stand out. From the start, Ubooly was primed to take advantage of two unique distribution channels—retail distribution (online at first, offline later) and app store distribution. We believed exposure to Ubooly through multiple channels would help scale the Ubooly brand. Additionally, each channel offered its own revenue stream. Through the combination of physical product and software, Ubooly could monetize through the sales of the plush while extending the lifetime value of a customer through in-app purchases of lessons and learning packs.

In just a year since we invested, Ubooly is available on four continents (North America, Europe, Asia, Australia) and speak five languages (English, Japanese, French, German, Italian). Early stage companies rarely operate outside the US at all, let alone have this broad of a geographic reach. Not too shabby for mobile-powered, cuddly creature from Boulder, Colorado.

team generally trumps a solo founder.

At Techstars, we've invested in over 500 companies. While a few of them were solo-founder teams, the vast majority had between two and four founders. And as we said earlier, we've come to believe that two to four founders is the right number, and that at least half of them should be focused on the product. A founding team of four, with three business people and one engineer, is a sub-optimal configuration, as the engineer will spend most of his time responding to the business people and the business people won't have enough to do.

The dynamics among the people on the team are critically important. Some founding teams consist of best friends while others are composed of people who have met recently. In any case, developing a constructive and effective working relationship is crucial. This doesn't mean that the founders agree on everything or have similar styles. Many of the best teams we've worked with have had plenty of conflict. The key is whether the founders know how to work through and resolve inevitable conflicts.

When investors evaluate a team, they look carefully at how the founders interact with each other. A team that doesn't have conflict may not have what it takes to make the hard decisions. The differences of opinion should be challenging enough to ensure decisions are thoroughly vetted, yet amicable enough to overcome the daily grind of startup life.

Harvard professor Noam Wasserman recently wrote a fantastic book on founding teams. *The Founder's Dilemmas: Anticipating and Avoiding the Pitfalls That Can Sink a Startup*[1] suggests:

1.  Bringing in co-founders who have the technical expertise, sales background, or social connections that you lack;

2. Creating a more diverse team gives you access to a wider, more diverse network (i.e., similar people tend to have similar networks);

3. Avoiding co-founding with friends and family; the eventual conflict far outweighs the value.

4. Creating a clear division of labor helps accountability and creativity to flourish.

5. Having a plan to address problems. Don't avoid conflict; make a plan for it.

As with serial entrepreneurs, a team with prior work history generates confidence for investors. YouTube founders Chad Hurley and Steve Chen sold their video startup to Google for more than $1.5 billion. So it is no surprise that investors (and media) paid attention on September 12th, 2011 when the duo decided to take over the flailing social bookmark venture Delicious. Similarly, when the franchise czars behind Boston Pizza, Jim Treliving and George Melville, took over Mr. Lube, the world noticed.

This might seem obvious, but investors like reducing the riskiness of their investments by working with entrepreneurs who they've "been into battle with" before. Investors can eliminate some of the uncertainty around how a founding team will communication and respond to adversity if the investor has previously worked with the team. You can help yourself as an entrepreneur by being brutally honest with yourself and your potential founders about how well you will actually work together and what the stakes are if you're wrong.

## CIRCA, by Matt Galligan (founder)

At the end of 2011 when Ben Huh and I conceptualized what Circa would become, it was extremely clear to us that reading news hadn't had any sort of leap forward ever, really. Sure there are more articles, they arrive faster, and we discover them differently, but at a fundamental level, the actual consumption experience was no different. At the core of the problem was this concept we called "news amnesia"—every day new articles came out that referenced yesterday's news and often times repeated a lot. This is called "background." But what if I didn't need that background? What if I still knew what happened yesterday? Every article serves two audiences: those who are new to the story and those who have been keeping up. Circa ended up pioneering something we called "follow" as a way to solve this problem and get continual updates on stories that move forward. We took our knowledge of the concepts behind software engineering, version control, and object-oriented programming and applied those principles to software for writing and reading news. Blending tech, product, and news content is still something out of reach for most news outlets.

While working through the concepts that would become Circa, we kept getting asked, and asked ourselves, a fundamental question: "Why hasn't this existed yet?" The idea was simple enough: make it easy for people to stay on top of the news stories they care about by allowing them to follow them, like people follow other users on Twitter. The more we dug into the problems the more we realized why no one in news had done it yet: because our solutions went against the way news was traditionally made, something that most of the industry and the people within it are completely indoctrinated with. We established early on that there was nothing sacred and that we should break down the ideas to their core and then build them back up in a way that we as consumers wanted. Our follow feature is still unique two years after launching because while the concept may be obvious, the barriers to recreating it are high, both technologically and culturally.

Everyone needs to be informed about the happenings in their world. News wasn't going away. But news was also not evolving. The structures for reading and writing were largely the same as they were a century ago. When evaluating what opportunities could be chased, how exciting would it be if we could make even a minor dent to such a legacy business?

INVESTOR'S PERSPECTIVE
## CIRCA, by David Cohen (Techstars)

A great investment opportunity stands out when it's the combination of the right idea and the right people to execute on that idea. Opportunities will often emerge out of long-term relationships that you've developed over time. When you gradually get to know someone, watching them learn and evolve and confront challenges, you get a sense of what kind of person they are. When you trust in someone's abilities, creativity and character, you can trust them with your investment.

Most seed investors invest in people. In Circa's case,

that person was Matt Galligan. He was in the first Techstars class in 2007 and since then I've gotten to know him very well. Circa was Matt's third company, and the third one that I invested in. After he very successfully sold his first company Socialthing to AOL, I invested in his second company, SimpleGeo. While SimpleGeo was not a success, Matt was a good steward of our investment and sold the company to Urban Airship, which has grown nicely and will produce a great return.

In 2011 at Techstars FounderCon, our annual founders conference of Techstars mentors and alumni, Ben Huh, CEO of Cheezburger and a Techstars mentor, had an idea for a media company and announced he was looking for someone to run with his idea since he was busy building Cheezburger. Matt jumped at the opportunity. It was such an awesome way to get a great idea off the ground and turn it into a reality. That's what can happen when you're able to leverage the power of a strong network to collaborate and bring ideas to fruition. Ben was a co-founder and was active as member of the board of directors of the company.

Circa is a clear combination of the right idea and the right people. Matt is very good at product vision and evangelism, and he put together an outstanding founding team of people with excellent track records. Along with the team, the idea and opportunity behind Circa attracted me. By capitalizing on the trend of mobile first, the product combines the way people use their mobile devices with news, content that everyone wants. The novelty of Circa is that it thinks about the news consumption pattern differently, allowing people to read news that matters to them quickly and at a time that is convenient.

It's a terrific idea and that was important in my decision

to invest, but the most influential factor was the relationship I already had with Matt and my trust in the people who would be in charge of making the idea happen.

## WORKING FULL TIME

Full-time commitment to the new opportunity matters. If the number of full-time founders is zero, you have a problem. Remember, ideas don't count. Execution counts and execution requires focused founders. If no one is working on this opportunity full time, how will it make progress? The more people who are all-in and working exclusively on the opportunity, the greater the chance that you have.

Working on a new opportunity full time demonstrates commitment. If you aren't able to do that, consider other ways you can show commitment. Investors want to see what is commonly called "skin in the game"—the idea that founders have something at stake in the outcome of the company.

Some investors are hesitant to invest in something that the founders won't commit full time to. But many founders need funding to afford to be able to focus on the opportunity, resulting in a big Catch-22. So what do you do if you aren't ready to quit your day job? If you can show that your product already generates revenue or users while you working on it part time, then you can make a credible case that taking on investment and going full time would propel you to greater success. While it's always important to show early proof of your concept, this is even more important when you aren't able to commit full time to your opportunity.

## BEEN THERE, DONE THAT

All great entrepreneurs learn from their previous mistakes as well as their successes. Experience comes in many forms, including leading a startup through a successful exit as well as getting a startup off the ground only to have it crash and burn.

Different founders have different experiences. By building a team that has a diverse set of backgrounds and experiences, you can accelerate the opportunity evaluation process since each founder brings different lessons to the party.

This is especially important in situations where you are a first-time founder. Rather than try to figure out everything by yourself, find a co-founder who has some experience. If you are a first-time founding team, find mentors who can work with you from the very beginning of the business. If you don't have experience, attract it, and include it in what you are doing.

Investors often say, "I don't want founders learning on my dime." While many investors feel that backing an experienced entrepreneur is a safer investment, others love to work with first-time entrepreneurs. While experienced entrepreneurs are often viewed as having more realistic projections and timelines, better access to resources including capital, and more seasoned judgment, first-time entrepreneurs will often be more creative and not constrained by prior experience. The combination of first-time and experienced entrepreneurs on the same team can be magical.

## PASSION

Starting a business is extremely hard. Resources are scarce. Obstacles abound. Success is elusive. The only guarantee in a startup is that you will have to work hard all the time for many years.

Entrepreneurship is a calling, not a job. You should only work on opportunities you are extremely passionate about. A famous golfer once said that people only do their best at things they enjoy. This is true as much for entrepreneurship as it is for sports. Passion for profits is not enough to keep you going in the middle of the night.

Solving problems that you yourself have—scratching your own itch—is a powerful approach. Michael Petrov, co-founder of Couple, a successful app that allows two people in a relationship to privately and securely share intimate communications, was born of personal need. While Michael's founders were at Y Combinator building the initial prototype for Couple (originally called Pair), their girlfriends were back in Canada and Japan. The strains of a long distance relationship led the Canadian founders to focus on creating a platform for connection with their girlfriends. This idea resonated so much that within the first four days of the beta launch of the app they had over 50,000 downloads and had facilitated more than 1 million messages. When interviewed on Sean's *Naked Entrepreneur* show,[2] Michael was asked how young student founders can find their passion. His response was laser-focused; he told the student audience to focus on their fervor. Explore and build what you would do on Thursday night if you weren't going out to be social at the university pub.

Founders will invest many thousands of hours into building their company. Before doing so, ensure you are going to love—not like—the idea. If you choose your opportunity based on potential monetary gain, what will you do when that money doesn't arrive? Instead, choose your opportunity based on what you are obsessed about.

The notion of "even if I wasn't funded, I'd do this anyway" is a good sign for investors. Matt Canepa and Pat Pezet from Grinds Coffee[3] had this type of passion. Matt and Pat raised money for their product, which is a coffee pouch filled with freshly ground coffee. They flavor the coffee pouches and supplement them with vitamins and nutrients. They came up with the idea one night while studying for a college exam and realized it could be a viable and healthy alternative to chewing tobacco.

Passion also has a dark side. Too little passion will undermine your *adversity quotient* (i.e., one's resilience to negative events) and you'll quit before you make progress on an opportunity. Too much passion can make you willfully blind to issues. Successful founders find the middle ground, resolutely believing their vision while staying grounded in the real world. The key is finding the balance between blind faith and rational optimism.

Jim Collins, author of *Good to Great: Why Some Companies Make The Leap While Others Don't* dubbed this balance the "Stockdale Paradox."[4] Admiral Jim Stockdale was a high-ranking military officer held captive for eight years during the Vietnam War. While in captivity, Stockdale was regularly tortured by his captors. Many of his fellow captives gave up hope and died, but Stockdale told himself he would one day be free and that he would someday get to see his wife again. But Stockdale balanced his blind and unwavering faith in future freedom with a grounded understanding of his current reality. It is this precarious balance between faith and optimism for the future on the one hand and acknowledging the current reality on the other that characterizes the Stockdale Paradox and it applies just as much to founders as it does to prisoners of war. To paraphrase Jim Collins in *Good to Great*: Entrepreneurs must retain faith that their venture will succeed, regardless of the difficulties. At the same time, founders must be willing to confront the most brutal facts of their current reality, whatever they might be, balancing commitment with critical thinking, blind faith with objective milestones, and passion with pragmatism.[5]

## COACHABILITY

Entrepreneurs require thick skin and resilient egos. Without both, founders would not be able to endure the ups and downs of startup life. All startups need both exuberant passion and stoic dedication. Without perseverance and confidence most startups won't survive their first year. Often all a founder has at four in the morning is her passion for the business she is creating. And yet, sometimes too much passion can be a barrier to honest opportunity evaluation.

Pristine Cart[6] is a product that sanitizes shopping carts. In this case, the grocery store pays for the product, but the benefit goes to the grocery store's customer. While the idea was clever, the opportunity was flawed because the cost to the grocery store was high and far outweighed the benefit generated, which was mostly goodwill from the grocery store's customers. While there could have been other approaches to Pristine Cart, the entrepreneur was stubborn and refused to acknowledge the imbalance of value, even after hearing it from several potential customers. Part of this stubbornness resulted from the entrepreneur having already invested $120,000 in the product. But when investors also tried to reinforce the feedback that was coming from prospective customers, the entrepreneur's continued stubbornness got him branded as not coachable.

Coachability refers to the founder's openness to external review, questioning, and advice. It is not about having the right answer but about being able to put one's own ego to the side and open up to external feedback. A great founder has enough confidence in her idea to actively seek criticism. This is a key part of the opportunity evaluation process, since being open to feedback allows an entrepreneur to identify and address potential issues with their idea.

Startups change and very few business ideas end up where they started. A founder who is coachable will demonstrate this ability almost immediately. To test coachability, a prospective investor may ask a direct question such as, "I'm concerned about Google, why don't you think they are a threat?" and see how the founder reacts. If the entrepreneur responds with "Google has no idea how to innovate..." it may be a sign that his ego is impacting his judgment and that he's not particularly coachable.

When exploring coachability, look for thoughtful, humble, and inquisitive responses. For example, when asked, "Where do you see yourself in the company in three years?" you don't want to hear something like "Leading the company. I'm the only CEO we will ever need." Something like "Wherever the company needs me" would inspire much more confidence. Or, in response to the question "Who on your team knows more than you?" a terrible answer is "No one." In contrast, a great answer is "Everyone. I always surround myself with people who have skills I lack." When asked, "I'm concerned about Facebook. Why don't you think they are a threat?" an appropriate answer might be:

> *Of course they could do it. They could do anything. But the relevant question is "Will it rise to the top of their product development roadmap in a timeframe where they could impact our go-to-market strategy?" Firms with almost infinite financial resources can do many things, but they also have structural barriers to rapid iteration around new ideas such as politics, bureaucracy and prioritization. Our laser focus and intensity around a specific, high-value idea is what will create barriers to entry in the wake of good execution.*[7]

Many investors aspire to contribute more than just money to a new company. They want to add their mentorship, their network and, most of all, the lessons learned from their own experience. Investors want to back entrepreneurs who listen as much as talk.

## 7 VIRTUES PERFUME, Barb Stegemann (Founder)

My passion stems from my gratitude that as a woman I live in Canada, a country where I can freely vote, I can earn money, I am safe, our children can go to public school, our roads are paved, and the list goes on. Raised in humble roots, on welfare for much of my teenaged years, I realized I could get a part-time job, and I could get clothes like the other kids so I could fit in. I also feel we must share what we have with others in a dignified way. I never wanted charity; I wanted to be invited to the banquet. So that is what I have created with The 7 Virtues. We invite our suppliers from Haiti, Rwanda, Afghanistan, and the Middle East to come to the banquet through our purchases of their essential oils for our fragrances. We are equals. I need them and they need me.

I am passionate about The 7 Virtues because it has provided me and everyone who loves our fragrance collection with a way to also empower families in rebuilding nations. I deeply appreciate my investor, W. Brett Wilson, who has become my mentor and gives me all the support and room I need to expand and grow our company. We have demonstrated that social enterprise can be excellent, and yet our products are extraordinary by themselves. And that's key for us—that our customers want our fragrances because they do not contain phthalates or parabens and they are vegan. Women tell me they could not wear fragrance before our collection with natural essential oils and they now are wearing it at work!

My passion makes The 7 Virtues a success simply because I respect this idea as much as I respect and value building your opportunity. Domain knowledge starts with knowing your customer and your industry. Do you understand what the customer wants? Do you know how your customer buys? Do you understand which features and benefits are most important to your customer? Do you understand the industry you are operating in, and know about—or at least have hypotheses about—the specific opportunities to disrupt the way the industry traditionally works?

If you want to run a startup that revolutionizes banking, domain knowledge would come in the form of years of experience working in the financial sector, preferably in banking. If you are trying to implement something new, having inside knowledge of how things work in that industry is an important starting point.

In the banking example, a person who previously was the COO of Bank of America wouldn't necessarily have the requisite business acumen, since they have large-company, rather than startup, experience. But they would have strong domain knowledge at a software firm trying to revolutionize the back-end processing of electronic banking transfers.

Domain knowledge can also help identify and attract key people as well as help ensure the startup's go-to-market plan is reasonable and realistic. For example, an executive who has spent two decades in the wireless payment industry will likely know what clients will want and what some of the industry's fatal flaws are.

Without domain knowledge, startups run the risk of building a solution that no one wants, often referred to as a solution in search of a problem. Worse yet, without domain knowledge, many startups oversimplify their problem analysis and dramatically underestimate the challenge of building something compelling.

## OPERATIONAL EXPERIENCE

The third corner of the Talent Triangle is *operational experience*.

Entrepreneurs with operational experience know how to make and deliver a product to a customer. In an online grocery store, this entrepreneur would supervise not only the creation of the e-commerce front-end website but also the process for the delivery of the food. Operational experience is all about getting the product from design to delivery.

Without operational experience, founders often have trouble launching their product. Or worse yet, they may launch but fail to deliver on their promises. A great product is only great if it reaches end users and customers. If your team lacks operational experience, look for people to add to your team who have built similar products in the past.

Albert and Richard Amini are doctors looking to build a product called Rolodoc[10] for the medical industry. Rolodoc is a directory of physicians and medical professionals for patients that allows for communication and rapid exchange of ideas. Being medical practitioners themselves gives the founders the domain knowledge they feel they need to take Rolodoc to market. While the Sharks agree that being part of the target market is helpful, the Rolodoc team loses investors when it comes to operational experience. Neither of the founders know the first thing about building, launching, growing, and sustaining a social network business.

## MENTORS

*Mentors*, typically experienced entrepreneurs or domain experts, can help entrepreneurs in a wide variety of ways including identifying issues before they arise, crafting solutions to obstacles based on prior experience, providing a role model for the founder to emulate, and acting as a decision-making sounding board.[11]

Limited resources often prevent entrepreneurs from hiring employees or outsourcing the many tasks they must accomplish, such as marketing, product development, accounting, and human resource management. Novice entrepreneurs must also rapidly develop management skills, a lack of which is often identified as one of the main reasons for a business's failure. Mentors can play a key role in these areas, as informal learning and coaching plays an especially important role in the growth of the skills of an entrepreneur.

Being a founder or a CEO of startup can be extremely lonely, frustrating, and full of conflict and disappointment. Simply having a friendly, safe person to talk to about difficult issues can be amazingly helpful.

## BOARD OF DIRECTORS/ADVISORS

Entrepreneurship has many maxims that seem to present the entrepreneur with no way out. It's frequently said that in order to raise money, you need a great team. But in order to have a great team, you need capital. This lack of capital dynamic often inhibits a startup from attracting top full-time employees, leaving the startup's Talent Triangle incomplete.

A good board of directors or board of advisors can help with this and other things, including:

- Providing a sounding board for founders
- Giving regular feedback on issues and initiatives
- Expanding the entrepreneur's network, leadership skills, and expertise
- Signaling to the world that the new venture is worth supporting

This last point is worth exploring further. In economics, *signaling theory* deals with how one party credibly conveys information about itself to another party.[12] By creating a board of well-regarded people, you signal that the company is worth supporting. When

Meg Whitman, the chief executive of Hewlett-Packard and the former chief executive of eBay, joined the board of Zaarly, a startup connecting errands with those available to undertake them, it signaled to the market that Zaarly was an interesting company. Most people assume Whitman, who led eBay to become a worldwide e-commerce success story, knows something about Zaarly's business and by joining the company as a board member she is implicitly endorsing it. However, don't follow this approach blindly, since simply having a famous executive join your board doesn't guarantee anything. Founders must still build the business.

A board of directors is elected by the shareholders. Directors have what is referred to as a *fiduciary duty* to the company and have a set of formal and legal responsibilities that is discussed in detail in Brad's book *Startup Boards: Getting the Most Out of Your Board of Directors*.[13] The CEO of a startup, regardless of whether or not they are a founder, reports to the board of directors, although there are plenty of cases where a founder can still control the board. Ultimately, directors can be liable for certain actions of the company, so they have to take their duties seriously.

Advisors can play a similar role to directors, but without the liability. They don't have the same fiduciary duty to the company, and rarely have any formal or legal exposure to the actions of the company. In addition, the founders and the CEO can add or remove advisors at their discretion as the board of advisors works for the founders or CEO, rather than the other way around.

## CUSTOMERS

One of the greatest paradigm shifts in entrepreneurship over the last two decades is the role of the customer in new company creation. During the dot-com boom of the late '90s, investors were seen as the proof of concept. Instead of being fuel, funding was considered validation and many entrepreneurs spent much of

their time seeking capital. Now, less than twenty years later, customers, not investors, are king.

There are many reasons why a founder should focus on customers, most notably that customers provide proof of demand for what you are creating. When a customer is willing to pay for your solution, even in prototype form, it demonstrates an unmet market need and can provide an amazing source of early feedback.

Today, the founder's credo has become "launch early, launch often." Steve Blank and Eric Ries have popularized this idea with Steve's mantra "get out of the building" echoing throughout startups all over the world. Steve is quick to say that "no product survives first contact with customers," so instead of concocting what you think is the most brilliant solution to a problem in secret, dump this approach and get your product or service out in front of customers as early and as often as possible.

From this perspective, customers become an important part of your early team. Accessing early evangelist users, early adopters, or beta testers has become an art form itself, with many recent founders leveraging a concept now referred to as *growth hacking*.[14]

To recognize the changing role of customers, investors often now ask questions around early adopters, including:

- Can we identify potential users and customers?
- Can we access them cheaply and easily?
- What traits do users of your solution share?

In addition to being users, customers are now co-creators. When you upload a video to YouTube you are co-creating a product that you are simultaneously using. The idea of *user generated content* (*UGC*) has been so important to business that *Time* magazine named "You" the person of the year in 2006. Companies like Facebook, Instagram, YouTube, Amazon, and Google brilliantly

leverage their customers as an asset and a co-creator. UGC has spread broadly to all companies, and you now see major brands such as Mountain Dew, Frito-Lay, Nike, and Best Buy using their users to help them with the product development funnel and creative promotion of their products.

Customers have also become a source of key funding for many innovative products through a new approach called crowdfunding.[15] Pioneered by Kickstarter, many other companies including Indiegogo, Crowdcube, and BetaBrand have arisen to further engage customers via crowdfuding. These companies allow for individual customers to commit small amounts of money in order to endorse the creation of a solution. The Pebble smart watch is an iconic example, as the founders initially failed to secure venture capital. Instead, in April 2012 they posted their idea for watch that communicates with your smartphone to Kickstarter with a goal of raising $100,000. Within 30 days they logged $13 million of pre-orders, all without having produced the product. Mark Cuban, billionaire entrepreneur and investor on *Shark Tank*, recently opined on the importance of Kickstarter by stating, "Kickstarter should be a requirement for every startup. It's a way for you to create demand and sell the product without giving up any equity."[16]

## SOCIAL CAPITAL

While parts of your social network might be captured through your social graph on Facebook and LinkedIn, your true social network is not only limited to those people you connect with on these platforms but includes friends, family, and the entrepreneur you met at the dog park.

*Social capital* refers to the goodwill contained within your social network. Entrepreneurs with large amounts of social capital will be able ask for help and support from their social network, augmenting the actual capital they have with social capital. Even if

you have plenty of money for your company, it may not have the same level of influence as social capital on convincing a reporter to write about your business or a prospective customer to do a pilot of your product. Social capital enables entrepreneurs to leverage their relationships to help move their startup forward and make better use of scarce financial resources.

Today, there is growing literature around the concept of social networks. In the last few decades this literature has explored the benefits and uses of social networks. For example, Mark Granovetter explored how social networks impact job hunting.[17] Granovetter found the majority of job leads came not from your friends and family (e.g., your strong ties) but from friends of your friends (e.g., your weak ties). This became known as the *strength of weak ties theory*, which suggests that you and your friends and family have access to similar information, while weak ties have access to knowledge outside of your social network.

Entrepreneurs who act as social network nodes with lots of weak connections bring in new information and many strong connections that can help signal success and result in an ability to obtain key resources such as talent. Investors will be more likely to back these entrepreneurs with a proven track record of being able to leverage social capital through social networks.

Investors like to back founders who are both known and in the know. Having a member of your startup who is widely known leads to better media attention and increases how others view your startup. These well-known people can be advisors, directors, or investors in your startup and will add to your social capital. Investors will view this as a powerful resource for your company.

1.  From "A Book in Five Minutes," *Tech Cocktail*, October 14, 2013, http://tech.co/founders-dilemmas-noam-wasserman-2013-10

2.  The Naked Entrepreneur Show with Professor Sean Wise, February 3, 2013 episode featuring Michael Petrov, http://nakedentrepreneur.blog.ryerson.ca/2012/02/03/episode-video-michael-petrov-acquiring-users/

3.  *Shark Tank*: Season 4, Episode 10.

4.  Jim Collins, *Good to Great: Why Some Companies Make the Leap...and Others Don't* (Random House, 2001).

5.  Marten Mikos gives a great interview on this at: http://www.youtube.com/watch?v=KpgnyBD9J5g

6.  *Dragons' Den*: Season 3, Episode 4.

7.  Thanks to Roger Ehrenberg from IA Ventures, who posted this answer to Quora. http://www.quora.com/When-pitching-to-an-investor-how-does-one-answer-the-question-Whats-to-stop-Facebook

8.  Sean Wise, "The Talent Triangle," *Globe and Mail*, May 17, 2006, http://www.theglobeandmail.com/report-on-business/the-talent-triangle/article1099632/?page=1

9.  Sean Wise and Madelon Crothers, "Debbie Travis, Reigning Queen Of Renovations: An Entrepreneurial Case Study On Finding Your Hedgehog," *Journal of Business Case Studies* (JBCS), 10(4) (2014): 363-370.

10. *Dragons' Den*: Season 3, Episode 10.

11. *Shark Tank*: Season 5, Episode 1.

12. Etienne St-Jean and Josée Audet, "The role of mentoring in the learning development of the novice entrepreneur," *International Entrepreneurship and Management Journal*, 8(1) (2012): 119-140.

13. Brad Feld & Mahendra Ramsinghani, *Startup Boards: Getting the Most Out of Your Board of Directors* (Wiley, 2013).

14. Brian L. Connelly and others, "Signaling Theory: A Review and Assessment," *Journal of Management*, 37(1) (2011): 39-65.

15. For a good overview on growth hacking, read Ryan Holiday's book, *Growth Hacker Marketing: A Primer on the Future of PR, Marketing, and Advertising*.

16. Max Nisen, "Mark Cuban: 'Kickstarter Should Be A Requirement For Every Startup,'" *Business Insider*, January 4, 2013, http://www.businessinsider.com/cuban-kickstarter-should-be-a-requirement-for-startups-2013-1

17. Mark S. Granovetter, "The Strength of Weak Ties," *American Journal of Sociology*, 78(6) (1973): 1.

# CHAPTER 4

# PAIN

"IS YOUR PRODUCT A VITAMIN OR AN ASPIRIN?" is a long-standing startup question. Josh Linkner, managing partner of Detroit Venture Partners, explains on his blog that vitamins increase health but lack immediacy. As a result, vitamins are optional for most people. In contrast, aspirin solves immediate, painful problems and subsequently is much easier to sell. According to Josh:

> *Businesses that service burning demand and visceral human needs tend to accelerate faster and require far less marketing push than those that offer stuff customers can easily live without.*[1]

In economics the difference between vitamins and aspirin is illustrated by the *price elasticity of demand*, which explains the variance in the quantity of a product demanded at a certain price. As a product's price rises, one generally sees fewer units of the product purchased. When price greatly influences demand, economists say the demand for such a product has high elasticity. Ice cream, fashionable shoes, and real estate all have high elasticity. In contrast, the demand for some products, such as water, air, and basic food is highly inelastic.

Elasticity relates to both price and demand. The more inelastic the demand for a product, the more a buyer will be willing to pay to acquire it. For example, your need to breathe makes the demand for oxygen incredibly inelastic. You would pay any price to breathe. Now, oxygen is omnipresent even though there is inelastic demand. The extraordinary supply results in the price being effectively free except in situations where there is no oxygen available. In those situations, you'd pay any price to get some.

If the demand for a product is elastic, then the demand will be very sensitive to price. Consider ice cream. You are probably willing to pay a range of $1 to $5 for an ice cream cone, depending on the brand and amount that is stuffed in the cone. But it's unlikely there is any reasonable scenario where you would pay $100 for the same ice cream cone.

Aaron Marino's product, Alpha M, is a set of DVDs focused on helping men improve their image.[2] Although Aaron identified men seeking a better image as an opportunity, he mistakenly believed his solution was an aspirin and not a vitamin. The Sharks didn't agree and informed Aaron that his DVD set is a "nice to have" not a "need to have." They felt the price tag of $297 was too high for them to believe the product would sell.

The demand for aspirin is less elastic than the demand for vitamins. Aspirin is something you need when you have an issue that requires it. In contrast, vitamins are "nice to have" but not necessary. Aspirin is a pull product, where the customer demands the product. In contrast, vitamins are a push product, where extensive marketing is required to push the product to the consumer.

Juli Deveau and Ozma Khan created Kookn' Kap, a modern version of the traditional chef hat.[3] Kookn' Kap keeps the smell of food out of a chef's hair and keeps the chef's hair out of your food. Juli and Ozma's product solved a small problem for a small niche market, which might be fine as a second stream of income, but in its current configuration it isn't a fundable business. Kookn' Kap isn't a bad product or poor solution, it just has a small market with minimal growth potential. A business with such a niche opportunity can be a successful small business, but it won't be a scalable or fundable one.

Contrast this with the idea behind Netflix, which is to allow users to watch unlimited video content for a flat fee without late penalties. To some Netflix is a vitamin that adds enjoyment to their day while to others, Netflix is an aspirin, solving the pain of late fees and desire for immediate access to content. In either case, it is an enormous market.

Value propositions are highly contextual, changing based on who you are presenting to and when you are presenting. In a down economy, aspirin is often all anyone can focus on. In an up economy, vitamins are often popular, as people are looking for new things that they don't yet know they need. But in any situation, aspirin is easier to sell than vitamins.

### COMPELLING UNMET NEED
Focusing on a clear pain point, or unmet need, is very powerful. The larger the pain, the more likely your product will resonate with customers. You can approach this as a low cost solution with a very large market or an expensive solution for a niche market. Either way, your customer should view you as a solution to a major problem she has.

In many cases, this pain comes from your own experience. Isaac Saldana, co-founder of SendGrid, calls this "looking for the pain."[4] Kevin Systrom and Mike Krieger, co-founders of Instagram, talk about fixing real problems, stating, "Every startup should address a real and demonstrated need in the world. If you build a solution to a problem lots of people have, it is so easy to sell your product to the world."[5]

Often, this large unmet need isn't always obvious. Drop Stop, a company founded by Marc Newburger and Jeffrey Simon, is a car accessory that plugs the gap between your car seat and the center console.[6] The Drop Stop can universally fit into any car or truck and it will stop anything from falling into the hole between the seat and console. The Sharks were skeptical until they learned the founders have already sold more than 250,000 units and grossed more than $1.3 million in sales, showing there was a compelling unmet need for Drop Stop even if it wasn't readily apparent.

To scope the aggregate size of an unmet market need, ask three questions: First, how many people suffer from the pain you are addressing? Next, what is the intensity of the pain each user feels. Finally, is this pain felt once, or over and over again?

## SIZE

Without a large unmet problem, it is difficult to create a significant company. If the pain you are addressing doesn't impact enough people, or doesn't impact people deeply, it will be difficult to gain market traction. If current solutions are seen as good enough, then the pain may not be enough to justify the need for the start-up's solution. The number of potential customers suffering from the pain you are addressing is referred to as the *total addressable market* (*TAM*). But TAM is not the only factor in the size of your market.

Continuing with the health analogy, let's compare headaches to leprosy. The market for simple headache relief is enormous because the entire world population is susceptible to this inconvenient ailment. Leprosy, while thousands of times more debilitating, has a much smaller total addressable market, as very few people contract leprosy. However, the impact of leprosy is much more significant and the outcome of it not being treated is much more grave than that of a headache. While medication for headaches has a much bigger TAM, the opportunity to cure leprosy could be a much better opportunity because of the inelasticity of price and demand. Someone with leprosy will pay much more for a unit of medicine than someone with a headache.

If the unmet market need isn't solvable but only temporarily stoppable, the size of the unmet need becomes larger. An aspirin solves today's headache, but you don't buy one aspirin, you buy a bottle, because headaches return. This return of pain increases the overall size of the opportunity by allowing you to sell the same thing to the same customer multiple times. Consider a car and gas. A car solves the problem of travelling long distances quickly, but once you buy a car that need is met. Gas solves the problem of fuelling the car, but you must fill up your car with gas many, many times.

FOUNDER'S PERSPECTIVE
## DAILYWORTH, by Amanda Steinberg (Founder)

DailyWorth.com is the leading women's guide to money and business and the idea for it struck me like a lightening bolt back in 2008. At the time I was making $200,000 a year as a computer programmer, but had built such an expensive lifestyle that I couldn't afford to pay my mortgage. I hadn't saved a dime and I was angry that I'd worked so hard to thrive professionally, but was overwhelmed by financial stress. I remember around the same time talking to my friend Leah in Los Angeles who had just been appointed executive director of a well-funded non-profit with seven full-time employees. She told me she was still unable to pay rent on her studio because she hadn't negotiated a livable salary. Something had to be done for women in particular because our financial woes just didn't seem to match the success we were seeing in other areas of life.

As an entrepreneur in my 20s, I learned repeatedly that businesses only succeed when they solve real problems in the marketplace. I was having too many conversations with myself and women friends about our struggles with money despite our advanced degrees, tireless work ethic, and grandiose ambitions. For an entrepreneur searching for big social problems to solve through business, the signals were too loud for me to ignore. So, instead of talking, or continuing to complain about the problem, I decided to do something about it.

I've started six businesses in the last dozen years. Two of them reached over $500,000 in revenue, but didn't scale, so I shut them down. The other three failed due to lack of user adoption. DailyWorth, the sixth, was attractive because it had everything a business needed to succeed: a real problem to solve, a huge, untapped market, a proven and rapidly scalable business model, and a clear path to revenue.

INVESTOR'S PERSPECTIVE

## DAILYWORTH, by Joanne Wilson (Angel Investor)

I was just starting to make investments. Maybe I had made a handful at the point where I met Amanda. I wasn't sure I was even sold on the concept before we had lunch but my friend Howard Lindzon had invested and asked me to meet with her.

Our one hour lunch turned into two hours. This is the story everyone tells when they become hooked.

There is no doubt that her timing made sense as more women become responsible for not only their own finances but their family finances. Women are going to make more than their male counterparts at one point. All the statistics are there. Women need communities and conversation around this topic. It is a topic that has been essentially swept under the carpet and that works for men. It doesn't work as much for women. Women like to discuss, get feedback, understand and probe. The concept that DailyWorth would create a place where women could educate, discuss and get involved in their own capital made sense.

Yet it isn't about the idea. I invest in people. Amanda has built several companies. She is an engineer so she understands product. She can build it. Her tenacity, her intelligence, her ability to articulate what she was building and most important she had a fire in her belly. Actually she had an inferno. I said yes I'd invest before the meal was over.

I got involved, came to board meetings, and to this day still talk to Amanda and give feedback and advice. As for me, the concept that I should hold back before making another investment ended up to not be my thesis at all. My thesis is all about putting money into entrepreneurs that are hungry and passionate about what they are building. When I see that and have a gut that they will figure it out no matter what happens is what gets me excited. Of course I have to understand and believe in the business.

At the end of the day it is all about the entrepreneur.

an amazing array of opportunities to use software to create efficiencies, make markets, and change how industries
worked. Yet with every company, I needed to incorpo-
rate communications into some kind of business process
or application. Time after time, I never found an elegant,
flexible, and software-based means of enabling real-time
communications with our customers, our vendors, or our
users. It was never clear how to do this without buying big
monolithic telco solutions. We suspected that there were
many software people like us in the world, people solving problems in their companies who ran into a wall when
it came to real-time communications. We confirmed this
suspicion with early customer research.

When we sat back and thought about why we'd had
this need so many times throughout our careers, it became
obvious. Every company communicates—it's core to the
human experience. Whether you're communicating with
customers or users, between employees, or with your vendors, communications is what makes business happen. As
software people, we're rebuilding so many of the world's
industries using the web and mobile software. If you ask
a developer to dispatch an email when a certain event
occurs in their software's workflow, they'd say "no problem." But if you asked the developer to send a text message
or initiate a phone call, they'd stare quizzically at you. Even
if they could make the phone ring or buzz since telecom is
geographically bounded, solving the problem in one country leaves the rest of the world unsolved.

However, we didn't recognize the true opportunity
until a couple of years into the company, after seeing the
breadth of what customers were building and the alternative that they had been struggling with for years before

turning to Twilio. A picture began to emerge that telecommunications—a two trillion dollar industry—was at the beginning of a once in a lifetime transition from its legacy hardware into a new world of software. At once, it became clear that APIs represent the new dial tone in a software-defined communications world and that we were at the forefront of that migration. That's when the full breadth of the opportunity hit us.

Whenever I have an idea I bounce it off likely customers or users who have the problem I'm trying to solve. Usually, I would get a tepid response. If I see a trend, then I move in. But with Twilio, we spoke with developers and presented the idea of a cloud-based platform that made real-time communications an accessible technology. Each time I'd talk to someone, I'd see the gears start turning in our prospective customer's head as they connected the dots between our solution and problems they'd encountered in their previous experiences. After I had that experience played out repeatedly, I dropped what I was working on to pursue Twilio full time and have never looked back.

INVESTOR'S PERSPECTIVE
## TWILIO, by Chris Sacca (Lowercase Capital)

The publicly switched telephone network is a disastrous mess of legacy equipment and protocols. During my time at Google I worked on the founding team of Google Talk and learned firsthand how virtually impossible it was for a team without specialized training to integrate into the maze of antiquated interfaces that comprised the pre-fiber global telecommunications network. As we sought out experienced telephony engineers to work on this stuff, we came up short because many of them had literally retired after logging decades and decades at the incumbents working on infrastructure that hadn't materially evolved in years.

After leaving Google, I took a trip back to my hometown and was helping my dad, a sole practitioner attorney, move into his new office building. A local business had quoted him a couple thousand dollars to set up his phone system. Being mildly technical, I naively assumed that I could dedicate a few hours, get it all configured myself, and save my old man the two Gs. So, I go into his utility closet and am shocked to find a copper spaghetti of dozens and dozens of wires seemingly entangled at random. His office building only had four rooms! I was useless.

In parallel with all of this, I knew that mobile as our primary interface to the Internet was going to explode. I had previously run a group at Google aimed at disrupting the world of wireless spectrum and could see the geometric growth of wireless activity. I had also made an angel investment in Twitter and was advising the company and had a front row seat to the power of SMS at the consumer application layer. It was in that role that I learned how damn expensive it was to integrate text messaging into the service because Twitter had to pay hefty fees to carriers for transporting these otherwise simple messages. If you read up on Twitter's history you'll learn that SMS fees almost bankrupted the company. In this light, when I met Jeff, I immediately and deeply understood the problem he was solving. He and his team had done all of the nasty and hardcore telephony engineering so that any developer with a basic knowledge of HTML (read: poseurs like me) could effortlessly include an array of formerly daunting services into their stack. It was as close to magic as I have seen in the realm of code. One of the best demonstrations of this ever was when Jeff would use a mere ten minutes on stage to live code a Google Voice clone using Twilio's elements all while talking about the future of the company. Utterly jaw-dropping stuff.

From an investor's perspective, the opportunity to work with Jeff was dreamy. Here you had an accomplished engineer with truly exceptional coding skills. He had exited a company before and then spent time building stuff at scale at a big company. It was clear from day one that he was going the distance with this venture. This would never be a quick flip. He is light-hearted, humble, and self-deprecating. His positive attitude is infectious, and you cannot escape his passion for solving problems. Jeff is one of those founders who leaves you with the sense that the success of his company would be inevitable if we all just busted our asses. My only regret is not having a bigger fund to invest back then.

1. Josh Linkner, "Aspirin or Vitamins?" *Josh Linkner's blog*, March 25, 2012, http://joshlinkner.com/2012/aspirin-or-vitamins/
2. *Shark Tank*: Season 4, Episode 2.
3. *Shark Tank*: Season 5, Episode 3.
4. *Do More Faster*, Feld and Cohen (2010), p. 11.
5. Dan Schwabel, "What Gen Y Entrepreneurs Can Learn From Kevin Systrom," *Forbes.com*, June 27, 2012, http://www.forbes.com/sites/danschawbel/2012/06/27/what-gen-y-entrepreneurs-can-learn-from-kevin-systrom-interview/
6. *Shark Tank*, Season 4, Episode 20.

CHAPTER 5

# PRODUCT

STEVE JOBS IS FAMOUSLY QUOTED SAYING that he doesn't listen to customers because they don't know what they want. The actual quote is more nuanced.

*This is what customers pay us for—to sweat all these details so it's easy and pleasant for them to use our computers. We're supposed to be really good at this. That doesn't mean we don't listen to customers, but it's hard for them to tell you what they want when they've never seen anything remotely like it. Take desktop video editing. I never got one request from someone who wanted to edit movies on his computer. Yet now that people see it, they say, 'Oh my God, that's great!'*[1]

Many businesses operate under the principle that the customer knows best and that whenever you are working on a new product or idea, you should start with a lot of customer research, focus groups, and market data. Clearly this conflicts directly with Jobs's point of view. As a result, many entrepreneurs ignore the conventional wisdom, especially when they are working on new innovations.

Regardless of which approach you take, there are fundamental principles in understanding how and why your product will have value, especially if you are trying to enter an existing market and disrupt incumbents.

## THE 10X RULE

The *10x Rule* dictates that your solution has to be at least ten times better than current product options to overcome the position of the existing market leader. Being slightly better, faster, stronger, or cost efficient is not enough. Having an idea that someone will be willing to pay for is a nice start, but the way you make it so that everyone will pay for it is to focus on the 10x Rule.

Consider several 10x solutions. Email is pervasive because it is more than 10x faster than traditional mail, which is so slow in comparison that it is now referred to colloquially as snail mail. Wikipedia has over 10x more articles than Encyclopedia Britannica. Amazon has over 10x the number of books as the World's Largest Brick & Mortar Bookstore[2] (located in downtown Toronto, Sean's hometown.) The original Apple iPod held more than 10x the songs of any Sony Walkman. Remember the fast growing Instagram example from earlier in the book? When asked about adoption and the criticism that Instagram was a feature and not a product, cofounder Kevin Systrom told Chris Dixon during a TechCrunch interview: "You have to go after a small, targeted problem that you're going to solve better than anyone else."[3]

Google's approach to search was 10x faster than the incumbent search engines while generating 10x better results. Google Docs started off free, which was an infinitely lower price than the cost of the incumbent solution of Microsoft Word. The Amazon Kindle, when combined with Amazon.com's huge selection, completely disrupted the existing publishing industry by offering immediate access to hundreds of times of more books on a device you can now fit in your pocket. Being an order of magnitude better at something is a powerful lever.

This exponential level of disruption is referred to by entre-preneurial scholars as *creative destruction* and, according to Schumpeter,[4] it lies at the heart of true entrepreneurial innovation. Schumpeter theorizes that new exponentially better solutions are adopted so thoroughly that they destroy the existence of prior market leaders.

A powerful example of how the rapid adoption of new inno-vations creatively destroys existing market giants is the story of Netflix vs. Blockbuster. Netflix's business model was originally based on DVDs rented online, sent by mail, and which had no late fees. When Netflix's business evolved to always-available vid-eo-on-demand streamed over the Internet, Blockbuster's days were numbered. Why go to a video store? Why pay late fees? Why have to put up with not finding the movie you want? Why leave your couch to figure out what movie you want to watch? Netflix was rapidly adopted and within half a decade Blockbuster was bankrupt.

### RATE OF ADOPTION

The *rate of adoption* is a measure of the percentage of the *total available market* that have adopted the new solution. Disruptive technologies follow Rogers' Theory of Diffusion of Innovation, illustrated below.

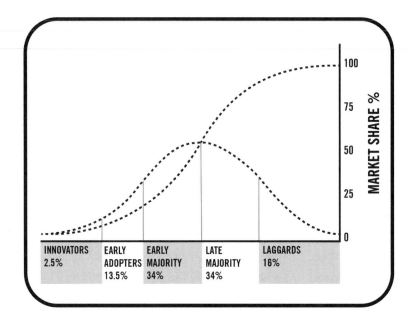

Rogers' (1976) Theory of Diffusion of Innovation[5]

Rogers' theory suggests that new innovations are not adopted by a population simultaneously. Instead, adoption of technology follows a definitive path for all innovations, where the time taken to reach market saturation varies. The adoption begins with the *innovators* and *early adopters*. This often takes a while, as the product is rapidly evolving based on customer feedback. The product begins to have broad applicability when it gets adopted by the *early majority* and is a market-leading product when the *late majority* begin to adopt it.

Consider Facebook as an example. The innovators were students at Harvard and a few other schools. The early adopters were students around the United States. The early majority were active computer users, including young adults and technology entrepreneurs. Suddenly parents started joining. By the time grandparents showed up, we were well into the late majority part of the curve. Market share grew rapidly but it followed Rogers' curve throughout the process.

Disruptive technologies follow Rogers' curve at different speeds. This pace is correlated with the price elasticity of demand and the 10x Rule since the more disruptive the technology, the quicker the adoption. Consider the charts below, which compare the rate of adoption for different technologies in the United States for the last century.

## NUMBER OF YEARS IT TOOK FOR MAJOR TECHNOLOGIES TO REACH 50% OF HOMES IN THE U.S.[6]

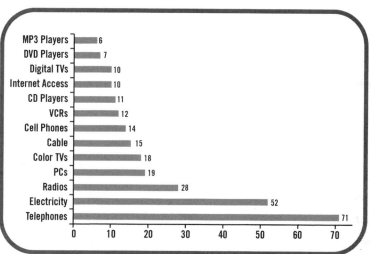

From this, you can see that:

- Speed of adoption of new technology is increasing—6 years for MP3 Players vs. 71 years for telephones.
- Technology is building on itself—we couldn't have the Internet without computers, which we couldn't have without electricity and telephones.
- The bigger the potential impact of the solution, the faster technology spreads.

## INTELLECTUAL PROPERTY

*Intellectual property* (*IP*), which refers to a set of legal rights that creators get, plays an important role in opportunity evaluation. An ad man can get a trademark on a cool slogan and that trademark prevents others from using it. An inventor can get a patent on a novel invention after which anyone who wants to use that invention has to pay the inventor for a period of time. IP law, in theory, is intended to spur innovation by ensuring the inventor gets the fruits of their labor.

IP protection is a subset of commercial law. There are many different forms of IP protection, including patents, copyrights, trademarks, and trade secrets, where the protections vary by the laws of each country. Depending on the type of product you are creating, different IP protection approaches will have different impacts.

A patent protects an innovation that is novel, useful, and non-obvious. Specifically, ideas cannot be patented, only the physical instantiation of an idea can receive a patent. A patent allows the owner exclusive rights to do a particular thing in a particular way for a limited time. After a set number of years, the patent will expire and the solution becomes public domain, meaning that anyone can reproduce it without permission from the patent holder.

A copyright gives the author exclusive right to the work they have created for a period of time. Copyright is most commonly applied to written materials, music, and video creations. Much of the content industry, and infrastructure around it, is built on the notion of copyright.

A trademark gives the owner the exclusive right to use a phrase or symbol. For example, Nike has a trademark on the phrase "Just Do It!" as well as on the iconic Nike swoosh. This is part of Nike's brand identity and can't be used by other companies.

A trade secret is any aspect of a business or product that a company decides to "keep secret" as a way of gaining a competitive advantage. Trade secrets are often considered confidential information and a legal document called a *non-disclosure agreement* is used to protect them when they are disclosed to another party.

Some investors argue that IP is necessary to facilitate commercial investment while others feel that IP laws are outdated and actually hinder innovation. In today's environment, the historical concept of IP protection, and the impact of it, is undergoing a great debate, especially with regard to patents around business processes and software.[7]

## KEY ASSET ACCESS

Some products require access to specific scarce resources. For example, high school gymnasiums can only be rented out to one group at a time. If a necessary asset to provide your product or service is scarce or, worse yet, dependent on access provided by a monopolizing group, you will be at a disadvantage.

The Vancouver-based company Hootsuite is an example of key asset dependency. Hootsuite is a tool to manage a person's Twitter accounts. Not surprisingly Hootsuite has a dependency on Twitter. If Twitter blocked Hootsuite from accessing its data, or even launched a similar competing service, the opportunity for Hootsuite might disappear. Think that sort of thing doesn't happen? It most certainly does. Many startups try to ride the coattails of larger ventures as a way of leveraging and benefiting from the popularity of the larger company. Sometimes, the larger companies push back.

On September 12th, 2014, Kevin Rose launched the app Tiiny to better create and manage small photos and animated jpegs. Tiiny leveraged the large community of users that enjoy and use Instagram through its "find friends" feature. At least it did until

Instagram cut off Tiiny's ability to do so just a few short weeks after launching.[8] This kind of technological protectionism isn't a unique occurrence. Facebook, which now owns Instagram, cut off access to its social graph for startups like Voxer and Vine who were starting to compete directly with Facebook.

Scarcity drives pricing. If your solution depends on the product of another, then your company is exposed to risk given this product dependency. If the product you are dependent on is scarce, the supplier can dramatically increase the price, resulting in lower margins for your product.

Scarcity can apply to direct resources. A call center typically requires access to minimum wage employees. A mobile software app developer requires programmers with knowledge and experience with mobile software. A shortage of either of these human resources would exert downward pressure on profit margins.

### PROOF OF CONCEPT—SELLING YOUR PRODUCT IN ADVANCE OF MAKING IT

All entrepreneurs believe in the potential success of their product. To gain an objective perspective, investors often seek evidence that the product is valuable. When Jackie Courtney pitched her business, Nearly Newlywed,[9] she had to convince investors that women would buy secondhand wedding dresses. While Jackie was able to produce third-party validation of her opportunity in the form of articles from the *Washington Post* and *Inc.* magazine, when she pitched investors on *Shark Tank*, she only had four sales in 30 days. While stories in magazines are nice, they are not proof of concept. Investors want to see early customer adoption, usage, and sales.

This is especially powerful if you can get customers to sign up for your product even before it is built. While it's challenging to get someone to buy something before it's ready, the explosion of Kickstarter and entrepreneurs running crowdfunding campaigns in advance of building their products demonstrates that it can be done. A more mundane example is a condominium builder who sells units before a shovel has broken ground. All that is needed are beautiful concept pictures, an empty lot, and a very good salesperson. In turn, the customer can purchase the condo at a discounted price for taking the risk that the condo may not be built exactly as promised.

In addition to confirming the need for your product, pre-selling your product has other advantages. You can collect cash from the pre-sales, which can fund your product development while reducing the need for financing from investors. You can also engage your early customers during the product development cycle, getting feedback from them early on to improve your product.

Prior to the dot-com bubble bursting a decade ago, proof of concept was analogous to the notion of flipping a light switch and seeing the light go on (i.e., the technology works). Today, more and more investors have expanded the proof of concept definition to be "turn the light switch on, see that the light goes on, and that the customer pays something to use it."

During an annual venture fair, where companies come to pitch a panel of investors, Sean once watched a bombastic venture capitalist loudly, and in a very public manner, inform a presenter as to the inevitable fallibility of their company. He stood up and yelled from the judge's table: "This is a stupid idea. No one will buy it. How do you even know anyone cares enough to buy it?" The entrepreneur's answer was calm, confident, and much quieter. The berated founder simply replied, "Because we sold 10,000 units in the first 90 days." Nothing validates proof of concept like actual sales.

## GROSS MARGINS

*Gross margin* is an accounting concept representing the difference between the price of the product and the cost of making it and is often presented as a percentage. For example, if your product sells for $100 and it costs $40 to make and deliver it, you would have a 60% gross margin. The phrase "strong margins" typically refers to gross margins that are both large and sustainable.

The dynamics of margins lie in two additional accounting concepts: *Average Revenue Per User* (*ARPU*) and *Cost of Customer Acquisition* (*COCA* or *CAC*). COCA is similar to COGS (*Cost of Good Sold*) in that they are both costs that increase as new users are acquired.

ARPU is the amount of revenue from an average user over a period of time (usually annual or monthly.) If you are selling a subscription service, the monthly ARPU would be the gross monthly sales divided by the number of customers. If you are selling business legal services, the ARPU would total revenue divided by number of clients served. ARPU represents how much extra revenue you make each time you add a new client.

COCA is determined from the total sales and marketing costs during a period divided by the number of new customers acquired during the same period. For example, if you spent $100 over a month to acquire ten customers, your COCA for that month would be $10.

The relationship between ARPU and COCA can get very complex and is dependent on the average life of a customer, which ultimately translates into *Customer Lifetime Value* (*CLV*).[10] While the absolute numbers of each of these will change over time, if you find that COCA is greater than ARPU over a specific period you have an issue.

As an entrepreneur, your goal should be high and sustainable margins, especially over time. While it's easy to talk about revenue, the money you really have to run your business is your gross margin. If that number is high, you have greater price flexibility, which in turn protects against opportunities that have demand elasticity.

In contrast, if you have low margins, you have to have massive demand to build a meaningful business.

If a grocery store buys apples at \$1 a bag and sells those same apples an hour later for \$2, the margin on apples is 50%. If that same store buys apples the next day for \$2 a bag and sells those same apples an hour later for \$3, the margin that day is 33%. In each case, the store only made \$1, but the risk was higher in the second case since the store would be out \$2 if they didn't sell the apples, versus only being out \$1 in the first case.

Tan on the Run,[11] a mobile tanning business, had made good profits to date and the founder was hoping to franchise her business. Investors were concerned that it would be difficult to scale her business because the cost to service each customer was high. As *Shark Tank* investor Kevin O'Leary told her, "All the cost of going there, setting up time, then going back, is built into your price. That means you're making 30% less than if I set this up on a corner somewhere. You're charging the same and you're doing all this extra work. If you had a fixed location you could line them up like cattle and spray them down."

A concept called *double dipping* can increase ARPU against a fixed COCA. When you double dip, you build the product once, acquire a customer, and then sell additional versions of, or add-ons to, the product to the same customer.

A great example of double dipping is Baby Loves Disco.[12] The founders, Heather Murphy-Monteith and Andy Hurwitz, toured the country in a custom disco van throwing incredible parties catering to families. The founders generate revenue from these parties in three distinct ways: ticket sales, merchandise, and sponsorship from family-oriented products. The more parties they throw the more money each of these revenue streams can generate.

Sean was able to double dip when he worked on *Dragons' Den* for five seasons. He was paid to support the show, paid again to give keynote speeches about the show, and paid again to transform his experience into content for this book.

## SCALABILITY

Scalability refers to an opportunity's potential to bring in revenue faster than the growth of related costs. With a scalable product, margins grow as volumes grow. Software as a Service (SaaS) products are often extremely scalable, as they can add new customers without materially increasing unit costs. In contrast, a law firm is not very scalable because for a lawyer to make more money from his revenue model, he must either: (a) work more hours or (b) charge more per hour.

Scalability has a lot to do with *variable costs*, which are the costs related to each unit sold, in comparison to *fixed costs* which are incurred regardless of the number of units sold. The amount of steel used by Toyota Motors is a variable cost. The more cars Toyota makes, the more steel is needed. A highly scalable business will have relatively low fixed costs so that the majority of costs are variable and scale with growth.

1.  Steve Jobs, "Apple's One-Dollar-a-Year Man," *Fortune*, January 24, 2000, http://archive.fortune.com/magazines/fortune/fortune_archive/2000/01/24/272277/index.htm

2.  Not surprisingly, there are several contenders depending on what you consider the definition of "largest" to be: http://retailindustry.about.com/od/famousretailers/f/What-Is-Worlds-Largest-Retail-bookstore-barnes-noblenew-york-powells-portland-oregon.htm

3.  Erick Schonfeld, "Founder Stories," *TechCrunch*, February 3, 2011, http://techcrunch.com/2011/02/03/founder-stories-instagram-products/

4.  Joseph A. Schumpeter, *Capitalism, Socialism and Democracy* (New York: Harper and Brothers, 1942).

5.  E.M. Rogers, "New product adoption and diffusion," *Journal of Consumer Research*, 2 (1976): 290-301.

6.  Census Bureau, Consumer Electronics Association, National Cable and Telecommunications Association.

7.  Brad believes the construct of a patent is invalid in the cases of software and business processes. See http://feld.com/?s=patent for a large number of blog posts by him about this topic.

8.  Josh Constine, "Instagram Cuts Off Kevin Rose's Photo App Tiiny From Its Social Graph," *TechCrunch*, October 4, 2014, http://techcrunch.com/2014/10/04/instagram-tiiny/

9.  *Shark Tank*: Season 4, Episode 10.

10. Much ink has been spilled over this on this concept. One of the best posts is from David Skok at http://www.forentrepreneurs.com/saas-metrics-2-definitions/

11. *Dragons' Den*: Season 9, Episode 8.

12. *Shark Tank*: Season 4, Episode 19.

CHAPTER 6

# MARKET

NOBEL PRIZE RECIPIENT Herbert Simon coined the phrase *bounded rationality*[1] to describe a view of human problem-solving ability. Since we have only so much brainpower and a finite amount of time to apply this brainpower, we can't be expected to solve all difficult problems optimally. Finding the optimal solution often takes more time and resources than would be, well, optimal.

As a result, it becomes much more rational for people to adopt rules of thumb as a way to get more out of our limited cognitive resources. Hence, *bounded rationality*, the idea that in decision-making, rationality of individuals is limited by the information they have, the cognitive limitations of their minds, and the finite amount of time they have to make a decision.

In the world of startups, a *bounded market* occurs when founders can identify the entire population of users easily. For example, the initial potential Amazon customer population, back when Amazon was starting out with the goal of being "earth's biggest bookstore," is bounded by literacy and access to the Internet. This was a large market, but it became unbounded, or one where the user populations are large, when Amazon expanded beyond books. Consider Google search, which is an unbounded market, in contrast to a search engine that only includes securities related documents such as EDGAR, which is bounded. Instagram is unbounded, while "the Instagram for doctors"[2] is bounded.

## MARKET STAGE

You've just created the best product in the world and it addresses an unbounded market. It's easy for your friends and family to learn about your concept, but how does the rest of the world find out? Unless you're in the movie *Field of Dreams*, "if you build it" doesn't mean that people will start lining up outside your house to buy it. You will need a strategy and approach to convince customers to purchase your product.

Recall from the last chapter that Rogers' diffusion of innovations theory specifies different groups of people who adopt new products at different points in time. Rogers classifies product adoption along a curve representing five distinct stages: innovators, early adopters, early majority, late majority, and laggards.

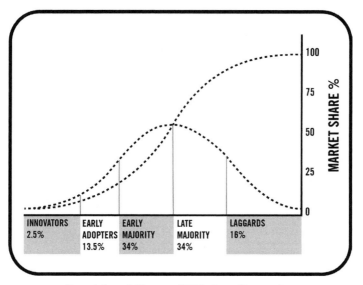

Roger's (1976) Theory of Diffusion of Innovation

Innovators, the first 2.5% of adopters, often require much more convincing than laggards, who buy because everyone else already has. During most of the 20th century it could take a product decades to move through the entire cycle. More recently, the time frame for these cycles has compressed, and it has become clearer which phase a particular product is in. For example, consider when you got a Facebook account relative to your friends, parents, or grandparents. The timing of this likely corresponded with the phase of the market Facebook was in.

While early adopters tend to be open-minded and willing to take risks on a new product, getting the early majority on board is often much harder. Yet the early majority are key to having a successful product since they represent a large percentage of potential users, and once they are on board the late majority quickly follows.

The early buyers of Tesla and Prius cars were almost entirely innovators. As time passed, the early adopters came out in force, at which point other car manufacturers began aggressively promoting electric cars and hybrids. While the "save the planet" message resonated with innovators and early adopters, as we move to the early majority, the message has evolved to include total cost over ownership, especially against the backdrop of high fuel prices, along with better and more contemporary electronics in the car.

In Geoffrey Moore's iconic 1991 book on innovation, *Crossing the Chasm*,[3] he begins with Rogers' diffusion of innovations theory and posits that a *chasm* exists between the adoption of innovation by innovators and the early majority.[4] Moore believes that innovators and early adopters are technology enthusiasts while the early majority are pragmatists. Subsequently, these groups have very different expectations when it comes to adopting innovation, which in turn results in a chasm that must be crossed.

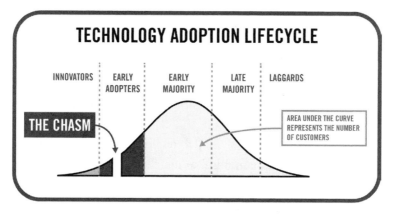

Moore's (1991) *Crossing the Chasm*

Moore goes on to discuss strategies to gain adoption by the early majority. These include:

- *Piggybacking*: When you buy a new computer, there is often a 60-day trial of an anti-virus program already installed. Without piggybacking on the manufacturer's existing distribution, the anti-virus program would have to rely on you to take the initiative to buy their product.
- *Industry Placement*: Viagra was originally intended to be a heart medication, then later branded as a sex-enhancing medication, leading to dramatic increase in sales.
- *Publicity*: When Virgin Mobile launched in Canada, Richard Branson arrived in downtown Toronto in a convoy of Hummers and beautiful models named the "Mobile Revolutionaries" who spread the word of mobile freedom.

When Greg Bay pitched Coretection to investors on *Dragons' Den*,[5] his original target market was injured athletes. The Dragons thought Greg's target market was too small to create a sizable business. Fortunately for Greg, he was able to partner with Under

Armour, an established sporting apparel business. With the Under Armour partnership, the target market for Coretection became all athletes, and Greg's product can now be promoted as a way to help prevent injuries and enhance performance. Coretection successfully piggybacked on Under Armour's already existing brand and distribution channels.

Each stage in Rogers' model requires a different strategy. Entrepreneurs must be mindful to match their strategy and available resources to the appropriate stage. If your product is too far ahead of the market, you will find it difficult to attract enough customers to justify your opportunity's existence and could run out of capital before the market warms to your product. If your product is too far behind the market, you may find your customers buying alternatives instead of what you have created. While having a group of early adopters buying your product is a great start, the real money is made by making your product popular with the majority. To get to the majority, you need to execute a reasonable marketing plan targeted at a specific demographic.

When a new model or approach to a business segment destroys pre-existing competition by offering a solution in an entirely new way or to an entirely new market, it is often called a *blue ocean strategy*.[6] The blue ocean strategy of creating uncontested market space is widely seen as the driving force behind many entrepreneurial success stories, including Netflix, Cirque du Soleil, Netjets, Curves, and the Nintendo Wii.

Charles Yim brought a blue ocean strategy to his product the Breathometer.[7] Yim wanted to dramatically expand the market for breathalyzers. Until Yim's startup, breathalyzers were only purchased by police and only succeeded in detecting drivers who were already driving under the influence. Yim felt there was a much larger market than after-the-fact DUI detection as he believed many people would not drive drunk if they knew they were over the legal limit before they got into a car.

The Breathometer plugs into the headphone jack of any smart-phone and uses an app to determine the user's breath alcohol content and correspondingly his ability, or lack thereof, to drive legally. In doing so, Yim created a new uncontested market, opening the segment up to anyone with a smartphone. All five Sharks decided to swim in Yim's blue ocean and he received $1 million in investment, well over the $250,000 he originally sought.

## PRODUCT/MARKET FIT

When evaluating an opportunity one has to consider many risks, including market risk and product risk. Up to this point we have largely talked about market and product as distinct concepts. The intersection of the two is referred to as *product/market fit* and is a milestone that every startup founder strives to reach.

Product/market fit occurs when a startup has found a product that the market will buy. This is rarely a perfect solution, but rather a *minimum viable product* (*MVP*) that customers are willing to pay for.

As product/market fit is the goal, an entrepreneur should have a hypothesis early on of what it will look like. Sean Ellis, a serial entrepreneur, has written on this topic[8] and asserts that if 40% of your early users say they would be very disappointed without your product or service, then you have reached product/market fit. A company achieves product/market fit when it has evidence that "sufficient demand in a defined marketplace exists to allow the efficient expenditure of capital to scale company processes such as marketing."[9]

Marc Andreessen, co-founder of Netscape and VC firm Andreessen Horowitz, who is credited with coining the term *product/market fit*,[10] describes this key turning point as the intersection of market pull and firm push. Pushing a product into market refers

The above illustration is from a 19th-century paper on microbes when S-curve evolution was first discovered. While the S-curve was initially used to explain the behavior and growth of a colony of microbes, it was later shown that the evolution of systems of many different types can be depicted on an S-curve.[12]

An S-curve is produced by the interaction of two processes:

1. The ignition and rapid growth of a chain reaction based on a positive feedback, or reinforcing loop, in a non-linear system; and
2. The gradual weakening of a chain reaction due to exhaustion of the resources necessary for it to "burn," or the emergence of negative feedback, or stabilizing, loop.

The application of an S-curve works for startups in the same way as it does for hurricanes and microbes. Startups with product/market fit scale up, leveraging massive adoption to generate greater economies of scale until saturation is hit, at which point adoption and the corresponding growth rate begins to slow and taper off.

The power of product/market fit is on display when Kent Frankovich demonstrates Revolights,[13] a product that consists of intelligent rings of LEDs that mount to a bicycle's wheels. Revolights synchronize to the speed of the rider to create a forward -projecting headlight that stays in the right position at any speed, a rear-facing brake light, and a dramatic increase in visibility from the side. Kent iterated on his product and used a single online channel to sell more than $600,000 of lights in the first year, demonstrating that his product has achieved some level of product/market fit before he went looking for investment.

## DISRUPTIVE INNOVATION

Most startups seek *disruptive innovation*,[14] a term coined by Clay Christensen,[15] which describes a process by which a product becomes initially popular in simple applications at the bottom of a market and then relentlessly moves up market, eventually displacing established competitors. According to Christensen:

> *An innovation that is disruptive allows a whole new population of consumers access to a product or service that was historically only accessible to consumers with a lot of money or a lot of skill.*[16]

# THE DISRUPTIVE INNOVATION MODEL

*Clay Christensen's Disruptive Innovation Model*[17]

costs, and unmediated access to actual viewers.

The Internet itself is a great disruptor of distribution. In the 20th century, if you wanted to access the world's encyclopedic knowledge, you had to go to the library and read the Encyclopedia Britannica. Now all one needs is an Internet connection to Wikipedia.

## CUSTOMER ACQUISITION COSTS

Peter Thiel, co-founder of Paypal, discusses the intricacies of distribution in his lecture titled "If you build it, will they come?" which is now available in his 2014 book with Blake Masters, *Zero to One: Notes on Startups, or How to Build the Future.* We borrow from Blake's notes[19] on Thiel's lecture with the following:

- Customer lifetime value, or CLV
- Average revenue per user (per month), or ARPU
- Retention rate (monthly, decay function), or r
- Average customer lifetime, which is 1/(1-r)
- Cost per customer acquisition, or CPA

CLV equals the product of ARPU, gross margin, and average customer lifetime. "The basic question is: is CLV greater or less than CPA? In a frictionless world, you build a great business if CLV > 0. In a world with some friction and uncertainty, you build a great business if CLV > CPA."

This math is at the heart of distribution. If it costs you more to land a new customer than that customer is worth, you have a business that will lose more money the more new customers it brings on. As investors, we often see CLV < CPA in the early days of B2B startups. The enterprise-focused startup will spend tens of thousands of dollars in direct and indirect costs to land an early customer, but that early customer will pilot the product for free.

Often this is acceptable in the short term since the startup needs the reference customer more than it needs the revenue, but it obviously doesn't work for the long term.

Thiel sums it up best with his statement, "Products don't sell themselves. Startups must find a scalable, repeatable, and sustainable distribution model in order to succeed, no matter how great their offering is."

## VIRAL MARKETING

*Viral marketing* is a tool for mitigating CPA. Each time a viral product is used, it is passed on to at least two other users, who each then pass it on to two other users, and so on. This process repeats until before you know it, thousands of users have experienced your solution. Andrew Chen, an advisor at startup Quibb, posted this solid tidbit on finding ideal distribution:[20]

> *You can figure out the right distribution channel by making sure the product has natural virality. If the channel in which the product spreads is new, you have a strong early advantage and can test the value proposition for new viral users and iterate with experiments until you see rapid acceleration. If you start with some initial traffic from a previous product, service, or piggy-backing relationship, you can accelerate usage quickly.*

Hotmail is the classic example of viral marketing. The original phrase is attributed to HBS Professor Jeffrey Rayport and VC Tim Draper, one of the investors in Hotmail. Each time an email was sent through Hotmail, a tag was placed on the end that read "Get your free e-mail at Hotmail." In short order this tag line was responsible for Hotmail gaining over 250,000 users each day.[21]

## COMPETITION

Every opportunity has competition. Your future customers always have a choice regarding how they choose to solve their problems and address their unmet needs. Competition comes in many forms, which we categorize as direct, indirect, alternative, and status quo. Anything your future customers choose to do, excluding buying your solution, is competition.

Let's take an example that occurs daily in homes across the United States. Suppose your teenage daughter comes home and proclaims, "I need a new pair of Nike soccer shoes." What alternatives do you, the customer, have?

- *Direct*: Companies selling the exact same solution/product/service, which includes a pair of high-end soccer shoes from Reebok.
- *Indirect*: Companies selling to the same customers a slightly different solution, which in this case could be a pair of knockoff soccer shoes on sale for half the price.
- *Alternative*: Solutions other than buying a new product. Instead of buying soccer shoes for your daughter, she could wear her older cousin's soccer shoes. This would meet her needs, but not lead to a sale for Nike.
- *Status Quo*: The "do nothing" option. Perhaps your daughter should simply wear the pair of athletic shoes you bought her last year?

Never, ever, believe that your opportunity has no competition. While status quo is often the most forgotten source of competition, it can have the biggest impact because it will always be the case that doing nothing is always an option. We've seen hundreds of businesses fail because the "do nothing" option was good enough for their potential customers.

If your customers have more choices, your product needs to be more compelling. Competition isn't necessarily a bad thing and can help validate the opportunity, educate early adopters, and define and differentiate your opportunity's value proposition. Competition can also provide a baseline against which your startup can be measured, illustrating the need for your product. When your competitors do a poor job of meeting customer needs, they will drive more customers your way. If your competitors outshine your business, they will undermine your sales efforts. Compare the postal service to FedEx and UPS. Who is competing more effectively?

There is no amount of ideal competition. Too little competition undermines investor confidence and interest. Too much competition scares away investors. Hot markets, especially ones being discussed in mainstream media, often attract substantial competition in very short periods of time. Many—maybe even most—novel and game-changing opportunities require being ahead of such mass awareness.

Companies that try to reposition themselves into a hot market based on the hype surrounding market leaders are called "me too plays" and aren't often seen as particularly interesting. One of Sean's colleagues is fond of saying, "don't jump on a bandwagon that's standing room only." So if your market is already filled with tens of competitors you should reconsider the market.

Future competition can lead to what Thomas McKnight calls *ambush exposure*.[22] McKnight defines ambush exposure as the possibility that an invisible competitor with extraordinary means and resources could find your product so compelling or threatening that they aggressively dive into your market and help themselves to your customers.

Disruptive innovations can create massively successful companies, such as Amazon, eBay, Facebook, and Google. But in creating of time, usually 20 years. When Larry Brun pitched the Attitube, a product made up of stabilizing weights filled with water,[24] he took time to explain the unique features of his product. Then he answered the question "Do you have a patent?" Fortunately for Brun, he did have a patent in Canada and the US, which gave investors the secure feeling that if they invested in the product the competition could not copy the technology.

Other examples of barriers to entry can include:

- *Cost Leadership*: Get your product at a cheaper cost, which allows you to sell the product at a cheaper price. Walmart is historically extraordinary at this.
- *Customer Loyalty*: Many people will only use Google as their search engine because they trust that it is the fastest and most accurate. To date, Bing has not been able to break through this barrier.
- *Control of Resources*: If you are making bamboo t-shirts and you have a way to control the flow of bamboo, then no competitor will be able to make bamboo shirts.

Barriers to entry add to the cost of market entry and therefore serve to enhance an incumbent's market position. For example, the airline industry has large barriers to entry. First, federal regulations are costly to meet. Next, the costs to acquire the equipment needed to launch an airline are extremely high. Finally, airlines must reach agreements with all the airports where they wish to fly. As a result of these high barriers to entry, incumbent airlines have a strong entrenched position and the airline industry is subsequently unattractive to many entrepreneurs and most investors.

When shaping your idea, improve it to a point that is dramatically better than any alternative and protect your idea by establishing barriers to entry. The bigger the barriers to entry, the harder it will be for a competitor to ambush you.

## GOVERNMENT REGULATION

Does your company require government approval or some type of government-issued license to operate? Many industries are regulated by some level of government and in order to participate in that market, a license may be needed. Government regulations may require testing, evidence, or even compliance with certain standards. As a result, government regulation can act as a barrier to entry and can significantly impact the cost to launch a product.

In other cases, government regulations may influence how and where you can sell your product. If you wish to open an institutional lending operation like a trust company, most countries require you meet certain standards (e.g., cash reserves), conduct business a certain way (e.g., can't loan millions to children under 18), and comply with filing requirements (e.g., monthly transfer reports). In some cases, governments restrict you from selling your solution to certain groups (e.g., anti-money laundering rules).

## PARTNERSHIP STATUS

Does your startup have potential partners? Do you know any of them by name? Do these partnerships materially increase either your confidence or the probability of success for the startup? If yes, then the venture is experiencing what scholars call the *halo effect*.[25]

The halo effect occurs when one entity—either a company, investor, or celebrity—tacitly endorses another by agreeing to work with them. Many startups use the halo effect as a form of proof of concept.

Under signaling theory, the halo effect caused by partners is seen as an endorsement. Consider the following:

*Startup XYZ is in the search industry. They claim to have invented a way to search images, something the search industry has struggled to address for a long time. On day one, they pitch investors "the solution to image search," but the live demo fails and investors lose confidence in the opportunity. The next day, the founders of startup XYZ announce they have entered a partnership with Google to leverage their IP and expand the market. Regardless of how investors felt before the announcement, Google's signaling and halo will raise the level of interest in the opportunity.*

While customers are the best testament to an opportunity's potential, what can you do if sales are not yet forthcoming or your startup is pre-revenue? In these cases, the next best proof of concept comes from partnerships with highly credible entities. Partnerships can come in all shapes and sizes, but generally the ideal partnership will see the partner allocating resources to enhance the probability of the startup's success. Partnerships should advance the progress of the company while increasing the confidence an investor has in it. After all, if a big company thinks your company has value enough to partner with you, then maybe there is something there.

As investors with a focus on digital startups, we don't know much about pharmaceutical R&D. But if a startup came to us with several large, relevant partners already on board, including a leading hospital, a well-known lab, a famous university, and a large public pharmaceutical company we would be more confident about the opportunity.

### KNOWING WHY YOU NEED TO RAISE MONEY

In order to realize the value of the startup, shareholders need an *exit*, a term used to define the moment that the shareholders, including the founders, investors, and employees, are able to cash out. Most startups typically exit in one of four ways: acquisition, initial public offering (IPO), stock buyback, or bankruptcy.

An acquisition occurs when another company buys the startup by acquiring all the shares or the assets of the startup. An initial public offering (IPO) occurs when a startup lists its equity on a public market or stock exchange. A buyback occurs when the startup has enough free cash flow to buy back the shares of investors and founders. The final and least satisfying type of exit is a bankruptcy. It's worth noting that fewer than two in ten venture-backed companies have a successful exit, meaning more than 70% of the these investments fail to return any money to the investors.[26]

Many entrepreneurs raise money to fund the growth and development of their companies. Some entrepreneurs want the money to launch a marketing campaign, others want to franchise their business, while some need to build more product. While it might be clear to the entrepreneur why they need funding, investors want to know how their investment is going to translate into more value.

It is up to the entrepreneur to effectively communicate how they can generate a return for the investor. If an investor asks, "Why do you need my money?" a bad response would be, "We need your $200,000 to grow our business." A better answer is, "Your $200,000 will enable us to fulfill a recent order of 50,000 units of our product. The gross margin from the order alone will total $500,000." With the first response, the entrepreneur is just begging for money, with no plan on how to spend it. In the second, the entrepreneur has outlined a clear path for the company to make a profit and build more value.

When early stage investors make an investment, they aim to make a substantial return, often at least ten times their money within a decade. One way they can make money on an investment is through dividends, which is a share of the profits, but it is unlikely this will total anywhere close to ten times their investment. More commonly, a large exit results from either the sale of the company or an IPO. Occasionally, investors have an opportunity to sell their shares back to the company, or to a new investor, in situations where the company has grown substantially.

On day one, all startups have the chance at a future exit, but some opportunities are more obvious than others. When a company has IP, market traction, and a sustainable competitive differentiation in a rapidly growing market with large barriers to entry, it is setting itself up for a successful exit. By locking up distribution, creating high sunk costs, and protecting key IP, a company can increase the probability of a successful exit.

Articulating the future value of your company to investors is intrinsic to your startup and should be the goal of all entrepreneurs. Likewise, investors want to invest their money, watch it grow, and then get back a multiple of what they've invested.

FOUNDER'S PERSPECTIVE
## TALBOTT TEAS, Shane Talbott (Founder)

It all started in my hair salon. I wanted to create a special experience for my clients so I shared my personal passion of creating unique blends of tea. My clients loved the tea so much, they kept asking to buy some. I gave away my blends, such as a green tea with strawberry and rhubarb, in small ziplock bags. My partner, Steve, encouraged me to use my creativity to create packaging and sell the tea blends in our spa.

Talbott Teas started as a business of leisure and shifted into a passion project. Over time, I realized that what we created with Talbott Teas was more than just a product—it was a brand of couture tea—a small, yet luxurious indulgence. Stores and customers showed so much support for the product that my partner and I sold the salon and focused on building Talbott Teas.

They say that there are no silver bullets in life. However, in a life-changing moment, Oprah put Talbott Teas on her last Favorite Things show, and Talbott Teas moved from being a small business run out of our kitchen and spa to a successful company with a more opportunity than we could imagine. However, our opportunity was met with serious funding issues. We couldn't fund the inventory to fulfill orders from major retailers like QVC, Four Seasons, and Bloomingdales. Trying to grow a business in the recession was miserable. Despite having huge purchase orders, every bank turned us down for a loan. So, we applied to *Shark Tank* in the hopes of getting an investor to follow the exciting trajectory we were on.

We went on *Shark Tank* hoping to get a deal with Barbara Corcoran thinking that surely she would appreciate what we are doing. We were surprised and not hopeful when we showed up to the pitch to see Lori Grenier in Barbara's chair. To our surprise, Daymond [John, founder and CEO of FUBU] was amazingly supportive but couldn't invest because he was invested in a competing business. Kevin made us an offer for a higher equity stake than we were comfortable with. We negotiated and despite him saying that he would not negotiate because he was a disciplined investor, he lowered his original offer and we made a deal.

Next to Mark Cuban, Kevin was the least likely Shark we could imagine who would show interest in a company like Talbott Teas. Instead, in his Kevin O'Leary "Let's make some money" kind of way, Kevin teamed up with Daymond to broker a deal with Jamba Juice.

Having two Sharks join forces after the show and help Talbott Teas get acquired by Jamba Juice was a dream come true. Never in our wildest dreams did we think that we would experience such luck stemming from passion, hard work, and a lot of risk taking. It felt like the best kind of luck—when opportunity meets tons of preparation. From Oprah to *Shark Tank* to Jamba Juice, we feel like we are living the American dream come true.

INVESTOR'S PERSPECTIVE
## TALBOTT TEAS, Kevin O'Leary, Investor (O'Leary Ventures)

I knew I liked Shane and Steve the minute they stepped into the *Shark Tank*. They were beaming with enthusiasm and passionate about their product—two of any successful salesperson's best assets. That said, I'd never make a deal with somebody just because I like him or her. I've met many business owners who come on *Shark Tank* with infectious personalities and amazing entrepreneurial spirit, but when it comes down to the bottom line, the money isn't there.

Luckily, Shane and Steve backed up their first impression with cash flow. After hearing that these guys grew Talbott Teas from $100,000 to over $500,000 in sales over just three years (with 50% profit margins to boot), I knew I wanted in. I always say, "The numbers never lie," and in this case, the numbers were screaming, "Invest, invest, invest!"

Then of course, there was the unique appeal of the market space. Tea is what I call a "recession proof industry." Caffeine is America's #1 drug and over time it has proven to be an addiction that endures any and all fluctuations of the economy. The only thing I love more than a business that's making boatloads of cash is a business that has the potential to continue making boatloads of cash for the foreseeable future.

I saw that potential in Talbott Teas and clearly I wasn't the only one. Just months after we joined forces, Talbott Teas closed a deal with one of the biggest beverage companies in America and was acquired by Jamba Juice. From day one, Shane and Steve were committed to their plan of eventually selling Talbott Teas to a larger company for millions of dollars, an exit strategy that I fully endorsed. They managed to make this happen sooner than anybody expected.

1. Herbert A. Simon, *Models of Bounded Rationality*, Vol. 3: Empirically Grounded Economic Reason (MIT Press, 1997).

2. Yup, this exists. It's called Figure 1. See Rebecca Borison, "There's Now An 'Instagram For Doctors," *Business Insider*, June 19, 2014, http://www. businessinsider.com/figure-1-instagram-for-doctors-2014-6.

3. Geoffrey A. Moore, *Crossing the Chasm: Marketing and Selling High-Tech Products to Mainstream Customers* (New York: HarperBusiness, 1991).

4. Stanley F. Slater and Jakki J. Mohr, "Successful Development and Commercialization of Technological Innovation: Insights Based on Strategy Type," *Journal of Product Innovation Management*, 23(1) (2006): 28.

5. *Dragons' Den*: Season 2, Episode 4.

6. "Blue ocean strategy" is extensively addressed in *Blue Ocean Strategy: How to Create Uncontested Market Space and Make the Competition Irrelevant* by Renée Mauborgne and W. Chan Kim.

7. *Shark Tank*: Season 5, Episode 2.

8. Sean Ellis, "The Startup Pyramid" from *Startup Marketing blog*, http:// www.startup-marketing.com/the-startup-pyramid/

9. Tristan Kromer's response to "How do you define Product Market Fit?" on *Quora*, April 7, 2014, http://www.quora. com/How-do-you-define-Product-Market-Fit/answer/ Tristan-Kromer?srid=uh2K&share=1

10. Marc Andreessen, "The Pmarca Guide to Startups, Part 4: The Only Thing That Matters," June 25, 2007, http://pmarchive.com/guide_to_startups_ part4.html

11. Marc Andreessen, "Product/Market Fit," *Stanford University EE204 Class Notes: Business Management for Electrical Engineers and Computer Scientists*, June 25, 2007, http://www.stanford.edu/class/ee204/ ProductMarketFit.html

12. G. S. Altshuller, *Creativity as an Exact Science: The Theory of the Solution of Inventive Problems*, trans. Anthony Williams (Amsterdam: Gordon and Breach Science Publishers, 1984).

13. *Shark Tank*: Season 5, Episode 19.

14. Clayton M. Christensen and Joseph L. Bower, "Disruptive Technologies: Catching the Wave," *Harvard Business Review*, January 1995, https://hbr.org/1995/01/disruptive-technologies-catching-the-wave

15. Clayton M. Christensen, *The Innovator's Dilemma: When New Technologies Cause Great Firms to Fail* (Boston: Harvard Business Review Press, 1997).

16. ibid.

17. "Disrupting New Growth through Disruptive Innovation," *Innosight*, http://www.innosight.com/services-expertise/expertise/disruptive-innovation.cfm

18. Peter Broderick, "Welcome to the New World of Distribution," first appeared in *indieWIRE*, September 16 & 17, 2008, http://www.peterbroderick.com/writing/writing/welcometothenewworld.html

19. Blake Masters, "Peter Thiel's CS183: Startup—Class 9 Notes Essay on If You Build It, Will They Come?" *Blake Masters's blog*, May 4, 2012, http://blakemasters.com/post/22405055017/peter-thiels-cs183-startup-class-9-notes-essay

20. Andrew Chen, "How to build a 'distribution-first' startup," *Quibb.com*, http://quibb.com/links/how-to-build-a-distribution-first-startup

21. Viper Chill, "9,000 Uniques in One Day: A Viral Marketing Case Study," *Moz Blog*, November 6, 2013, http://moz.com/blog/9000-uniques-viral-marketing-case-study

22. Thomas K. McKnight, *Will it Fly?: How to Know If Your New Business Idea Has Wings...Before You Take the Leap*, (Financial Times Prentice Hall,

Pearson, 2003), p. 89.

23. Harold Demsetz, "Barriers to Entry," *American Economic Review*, 72(1) 1982: 47-57.

24. *Dragons' Den*: Season 3, Episode 6.

25. See Richard E. Nisbett and Timothy DeCamp Wilson, "The Halo Effect: Evidence for Unconscious Alteration of Judgments," *Journal of Personality and Social Psychology*, 35(4) (1977): 250 and Lance Leuthesser, Chiranjeev S. Kohli, and Katrin R. Harich, "Brand Equity: The Halo Effect Measure," *European Journal of Marketing*, 29(4) 1995: 57-66. See also Phil Rosenzweig, *The Halo Effect:...and the Eight Other Business Delusions That Deceive Managers*, (Simon and Schuster, 2007).

26. Deborah Gage, "The Venture Capital Secret: 3 Out of 4 Start-Ups Fail," *Wall Street Journal*, September 20, 2012, http://www.wsj.com/articles/SB10 0008723963904437202004578004980476429190

CHAPTER 7

# PLAN

STEVE BLANK IS FAMOUS for paraphrasing Field Marshal
Helmuth Graf von Moltke on his blog and reminding us
that no business plan survives first contact with the customer.[1] Many mistake Blank's (and Graf's) instruction and go only
halfway. These founders ask their customers what they want. That
approach is not sufficient. Instead entrepreneurs should present
potential customers with choices and let them show their opinion
with their wallets.

There is a secondary message in Blank's warning, which is that
business plans are only a starting point. One has to execute on
those plans, and due to high levels of uncertainty, continuously
evolve and adapt the plan on the fly. Darwin was correct—those
who can adapt will survive, not just in nature but in the startup
jungle as well.

## LAUNCH EARLY AND OFTEN
### by David Cohen, Founder, Techstars[2]

A product that nobody uses is like a tree falling in the for-
est when no one is around to hear it. Maybe it makes a

sound, maybe not—but really, who even cares? The same goes for your product. It could be the coolest idea ever, but if no one is around to use it, who cares? If actual customers aren't using your product or service, there's no way to know what's working and what needs to be changed. Keep in mind that the product launch and the marketing launch are two separate things. Your marketing launch can wait. It's fine to delay making a lot of noise and promoting your company in the media until you have good product/market fit and customers love the product. But in order to get to that point, the product itself should be launched early and often.

Are you waiting for it to be perfect, or even respectable? Stop waiting. As Matt Mullenweg says in *Do More Faster*:[3] "If you're not embarrassed when you ship your first version, you waited too long." You need to get your product out there so you can get the feedback that will make it better. If you're working to create something that addresses your customers' needs and solves a problem for them, they'll probably be more than willing to share their opinions. Along with verbal feedback, the ways they use the product might reveal a specific need that you didn't even know existed.

Meanwhile, you're also developing and refining your customer base. Even if your actual product changes dramatically over time, those early customers can become your biggest fans and advocates. Then when it's time for your big marketing launch, there will be plenty of people around who care about the noise you're making.

## TIME TO LAUNCH

The longer it takes to launch, the more chances there are that something will go wrong. If you are hoping to build an application for the iPhone, then your time to launch ends with the listing of your app in the App Store. The longer it takes to do that, the more chance there is for a competitor to undermine your opportunity and beat you to the punch.

Many new companies focus on establishing a beachhead when they get started. A beachhead is a military term for establishing a foothold on the ground before launching a full attack. In the world of startups, a beachhead refers to a small, easily accessible and manageable initial target.

By establishing a beachhead, the startup is able to generate early feedback before investing deeply in a go-to-market plan. Facebook started with a small beachhead—a single university (Harvard). As Facebook expanded, it limited early users to those who had an .edu email address through their university or college. This allowed the founders to create a minimal viable product geared toward addressing an unmet need in a manageable target market—in this case, students—while establishing a beachhead to expand from.

To instill confidence in your go-to-market plan, consider which target market could be an ideal beachhead for you.

## PLAN TO SCALE

As an entrepreneur you are trying to find a business model that is repeatable, sustainable, and scalable. As we discussed earlier, scaling occurs only after a business finds its product/market fit. This normally is well past the opportunity evaluation phase, but that doesn't mean you can ignore scaling in the early days. If you can't figure out a plan to scale during the opportunity evaluation phase, you should not proceed.

Once you have found your business model and product/market fit you will begin to scale. This is a process where you add incremental revenue without adding incremental costs. If scaling your startup results in increased costs without additional returns then the company is prematurely scaling prior to product/market fit.

According to a recent report from the Startup Genome Project, the number one cause of startup failure is *premature scaling*.[4] Startup Genome estimates that 74% of high growth Internet startups fail due to premature scaling, which is defined as "focusing on one dimension of the business and advancing it out of sync with the rest of the operation." This happens when a startup expands too quickly, spends too much money on this expansion, and then finds revenue being outpaced by expenses. You can fall into the trap of premature scaling by overspending on customer acquisition, confusing early adopters with a larger market segment, or by shifting engineering resources out of R&D and into technical support too quickly.

Ponder this messy example:

Mrs. D. has invented a biodegradable toilet paper that degrades 10x faster than all other toilet paper. She files a patent on her product but, before going to market to see if customers want her innovation, she decides to corner the market on her paper's key ingredient. Doing so costs her millions of dollars but ensures she is the only one who can sell her product. A year later, she has cornered the market on the supply of highly biodegradable toilet paper. Unfortunately, Mrs. D. didn't conduct pilot tests or focus groups on her innovation with real customers. As a result, Mrs. D. was shocked to learn that end users don't like her product, so much so that her customers, primarily the large distributors of toilet paper, won't carry it since they already sell cheap non-biodegradable toilet paper. Mrs. D. has prematurely scaled her business.

## REASONABLE NOT RIGHT

While predicting the future accurately is impossible, it doesn't stop many entrepreneurs from announcing that their five-year future revenue forecast is conservative. Many entrepreneurs misunderstand the motivation behind investors' interest in future results. Investors prefer reasonable to right. Since it is impossible to predict your revenue in five years, entrepreneurs should spend less time trying to prove their numbers are correct. Instead, founders should understand and be clear about the assumptions that lead to these numbers and include them in their plan.

Josh Brooks from Postcard on the Run illustrates what happens when you aren't reasonable. Postcard on the Run[5] allows its users to send personalized postcards from anywhere in the world. You simply take a picture, write a message, sign with your finger, and send it off, all done from the convenience of your mobile phone. Josh demonstrates several aspects of an effective pitch, but he does not show the ability to be reasonable when making his company's valuation proposal. He states that for $300,000, the Sharks can have 5% of his company (a $6 million valuation). Given the very early stage of Postcards on the Run, Josh isn't being reasonable, and the Sharks chew him up.

Melissa Carbone creates live horror attractions. She has run haunted hayrides in Los Angeles and New York, as well as a haunted camping trip. Last year her venture generated $1 million in gross sales. While this impressed the Sharks, they were unimpressed with her valuing her company at $20 million along with her inability to articulate a rationale for the valuation. In the end, Mark Cuban and Melissa agree to an investment of $2 million for 20%, making her post-money valuation a more reasonable $10 million.

## THE ART OF FINANCIAL FORECASTING
### John Pinsent, CA, ICD.D (St. Arnaud Pinsent Steman, Chartered Accountants)

Effective financial forecasting is an entrepreneur's business GPS. Financial forecasting allows entrepreneurs to know accurately and objectively where they are along the route to success, where they want to get to and, most importantly, receive helpful instructions along the way. For first time entrepreneurs, the task of creating financial statements and the financial model that underlies them is daunting. Having never walked this path before, entrepreneurs often barely know where the on button is, let alone how to navigate to the nearly mythical exit that is their final destination. Fortunately, many prior travellers on the road to startup success have walked this path before you, although many of these entrepreneurs have also gotten lost along the way. But if you keep to the basics and stay the course of best practices, then you too can learn to navigate the highway of effective financial forecasting.

As an angel investor, your financial forecast is the third most important thing that I'll consider as I'm contemplating my investment. First, I need to like you and your team. Can I trust you? Do you have the skills necessary to build a valuable enterprise? Next, I need to really like your concept. Is it unique? Can I imagine people engaging with it and is it the kind of business that I would be proud to be associated with? Can I offer more than cash? Once you've cleared these two hurdles—team and idea—I turn my attention to your financial forecasts. Like team and idea, financial forecasts, while varied, can quickly help me make that all-important first decision: Do I want to hear more?

Why are financial forecasts so important? The simple answer is that the financial forecast tells investors a lot about you and your business. By reviewing your forecasts, we will learn a lot about your market, your margins, and your business mechanics. Through this analysis, we'll discover much of what investors need to know about how you are going to take my hard-earned money and hopefully turn this great idea into a healthy profit for us all. But we learn more than just the numbers from your financials. We also learn the level of business acumen of your team. Business acumen ensures that the financials are realistic, achievable, and based on grounded real-life experience and reasonable assumptions. You don't have to be right, but you do have to be reasonable.

Your financial forecasts also serve to set the tone for how the investment is going to be valued and what an investor's expected rate of return will be. If your forecasts are far off the road of reality, then you've sent me a clear message that you don't understand your business, your market, or your ability to capture value from both. If your financial forecasts are excessively conservative, then you run the risk of losing my interest by failing to hit my return on investment expectations. After all, no one wants to put $50,000 into a high-risk venture if the upside is only 10%.

Bill Gates often talks about how people overestimate what they will achieve in the short term and underestimate what they will realize over the long haul. He's absolutely right! The art of financial forecasting is finding that balance between operational realism and infectious entrepreneurial optimism.

If you want to impress a potential investor, I suggest all entrepreneurs keep the following things in mind as you develop your financial forecasts:

*Anchor in the present*: I'm going to intensely analyze the first year or any period that the current round of financing will cover. I'll be interested in knowing how years two and three are expected to play out but will put anything beyond those years down to pure optimistic speculation. The key is to anchor in the present and scale from there (e.g., we are projecting $100,000 in the first year and are pushing to double that in each of the following years.) Make sure the plan for the next year holds water.

*Forget the exit*: Unless you've built and sold a business several times before, I know that you don't have a clue about where this opportunity will take us. Don't be afraid to dream big, but know that the valuation for the purposes of my investment will rest on the details of the next 12 months.

*Bottom-up, not top-down*: Your financial forecasts have to be tied to your operational realities. If you are projecting sales of $2 million, then the assumptions on which your financial forecast are built must include staffing, advertising, travel, and marketing budgets that can realistically expect to deliver that level of sales activity. If you have product engineering work to be done, then the number of project hours needed to complete that work must tie into a head count and related staffing budget that can deliver those hours. Ultimately, you'll be held accountable for how investment dollars are spent. What your financial forecast should show investors is that your business will include an accountability framework that will ensure that your targets can be achieved within the timelines and budget dollars you are projecting. Remember, no one expects you to be right, just reasonable.

*Ask for directions*: While all founders have different levels of financial acumen, they should ground their projections in reality. One way to do that is to ask for directions. Solicit input on your financials from those who have more experience than you. Test your assumptions with future clients, with potential suppliers, and with advisors. The more you test your assumptions and adjust according to third-party feedback, the more comfortable most investors will be.

*Plan macro and execute micro*: Investors understand that it is very difficult to accurately predict the path that the commercialization of your product will take. I need to see and understand the financial framework at a macro level. The details and assumptions below that level should give me the confidence that you've thought of all those details through and have a plan to execute at that micro level. If you win me over on the framework, I'll give you the rope to execute at the day-to-day level.

*Fresh and evolved*: Keep your forecasts fresh and your assumptions fluid. If your forecasts are for the current year and we're already in December, they really don't have much value to me. Prepare your forecasts so that they can roll with your operational milestones as they are realized. Ensure that you can update your forecasts in real time to reflect operational realities, such as not being able to fill a key management role at the exact time you thought it would be filled. Generally, the software that you use to build your forecasts will allow for dynamic updates to assumptions and key input variables. Stay current with all of the key data points. Remember, you will be expected to ground your financials in reality. If you miss your sales target, you can't simply reforecast it retroactively to

Validation Board diagram with labels including: leanstartupmachine, Validation Board, Project Name, Team Leader Name, Track Pivots, Start, 1st Pivot, 2nd Pivot, 3rd Pivot, 4th Pivot, Customer Hypothesis, Problem Hypothesis, Solution Hypothesis, Design Experiment, Core Assumptions, Riskiest Assumption, Method, Minimum Success Criterion, Results, GET OUT OF THE BLDG, Invalidated, Validated, www.ValidationBoard.com

## PLAN B

In two decades years of venture investing, we have never seen a business end up where it predicted it would be. Things change, and innovative things change quickly. As result, every opportunity needs a back-up plan, a Plan B. In fact, have a Plan C and Plan D as well.

Ideally your product, solution, or service has multiple uses or user types. For example, billing software for law firms could probably also do well in accounting firms, but it might also be used for non-billing purposes. Understanding the various opportunities for monetization is key at the evaluation stage.

Things change. Competitors appear. Governments repeal regulations. Key staff leave. Your ability to formulate multiple plans for when the first one doesn't work is a key characteristic of a great entrepreneur.

## DISQUS, by Daniel Ha (Founder)

We started Disqus because we really cared about online communities. That is, the traditional understanding of online communities: message boards, forums, Usenet groups, and IRC channels. These are where the geeks and experts get together to share and learn from each other. That's different from social networks where people share with friends and family. Online communities, in our opinion, are at the core of what makes the Internet amazing. Disqus was started to explore how to unlock major value from this in a way that's never been done before.

Because the Disqus mission was personal to me, building the product and business was inherently an opportunity that I knew I could spend a lot of time pursuing. In itself, that makes it an opportunity worth considering.

To use Disqus, people install Disqus on their websites. That's all they have to do to get going. This approach to "online communities" proved to be successful for us because it allowed Disqus to very quickly grow a network. In a relatively short time frame, the network spanned millions of websites and billions of page views.

But the business opportunity was not always obvious to us. Initially, it was all free to use. Would people pay for this? Are we building a software service company? We tried a variety of models and began to narrow down to a core hypothesis. This was done by paying attention to how people used our products, as well as understanding what type of company it was that we wanted to build. Whatever business model we would end up pursuing, we knew that our opportunity was in a "community network" with unparalleled scale and reach. We knew that the company that we were building should have a revenue model that matched the ambitious scale of our product.

All of this is to basically say that we didn't have a true business plan at the very beginning. But because of the fast, sustained growth of our product's adoption, I knew that we were doing something interesting for a non-trivial number of people. The fact that it grew in the face of real competition meant that we were doing something right in our execution. Very early on, we outlined ways that Disqus could make revenue. It was important to consider a few different pathways, knowing that if we were going to build a valuable company, we would eventually have multiple products with potentially multiple lines of revenue. So the most important thing was to create a foundation that told us that we had true product/market fit.

The software-as-a-service model didn't work out for us. Not because there wasn't a market there; it was because building that type of business wasn't part of our core DNA. We didn't naturally do it well, and we didn't have much desire to try to do it well. If we continued, I realized that we'd be building a company that I didn't want to work on anymore. So we make a bold decision and abandoned this growing revenue line, and completely shift to another type of business: advertising and media. We knew that as a network with sufficient scale we had more than a product—we had an ecosystem that was valuable for many different parts of our market.

This was a more ambitious plan and one that's harder to execute on. But it was an opportunity that supported the original mission and would help us create the company that we wanted to keep building.

## DISQUS, by Naval Ravikant (Investor)

I met Daniel at Y Combinator Demo Day in late 2007. I'd been experimenting with viral growth applications at the time (it was still a relatively new framework back then), and I was impressed by how quickly communities could be built online. I chatted with Daniel about it at YC Demo Day and he struck me as quiet and competent.

Daniel was extremely professional—he followed up and smartly asked me for advice rather than for money. I went to see them in their apartment/office. It's striking how bad the state of blog commenting was back then. The Disqus product was light years ahead of the native commenting systems. I was personally using Squarespace at the time and as a nascent blogger, felt the pain. I also have a strong belief that every product is better when it's made social. The promise of the web isn't to connect people to computers, but rather *through* computers.

Daniel kept updating me month by month on the stats—never pushing or chasing, but not being silent either. That built up trust quickly. It also helped that the team was iterating their product quickly, and growing. They went from one million page views a month in October to 20 million in November to 35 million in December. Clearly, they were on to something.

The hard part with a product like Disqus is monetization. The scale required before you can monetize a conversational social app is enormous, so that was a big leap of faith to make. Regardless, communities are sticky and have huge value and it was clear that the blogosphere was growing, and Disqus even more so. At the end of the day,

## Q&A

While most interactions with a potential investor around a new business usually begin with an elevator pitch, they almost always end with questions being asked. The best investors aren't only listening to the answers but are observing how the answers are being given. Has the entrepreneur thought through the question or has she simply given a canned answer? Does she get frustrated? Do all team members presenting get involved? Do each of the founders give the same answers? If an investor disagrees with the answer and pushes back on the response, how does the entrepreneur react?

As discussed in the earlier sections on coaching and mentorship, exploring an idea is a dynamic process, one in which many mistakes will be made. How an entrepreneur interacts during Q&A can often shed light on the founders' business approach. Some entrepreneurs see questions as a way of exploring deeper topics of interest that the audience wishes to learn more about. Other entrepreneurs see questions as an attack on the opportunity. The former is ideal—the latter, not so much.

FOUNDER'S PERSPECTIVE
### NEXT BIG SOUND, by Alex White (Founder)

Going back to the early pitch, why was Next Big Sound a great opportunity? We had several factors working in our favor. First of all, we were positioned in a sexy, multi-billion dollar global industry. We found ourselves in the midst of a massive, well-documented disruption in the way people consume music. We faced a large, but slow, incumbent player in Nielsen Soundscan. There was general confusion in the marketplace about which numbers were worth tracking and how the music industry should navigate the digital world.

I wish that I could say that our pitch came down from the mountaintop fully written, but that is pretty much the opposite of what happened.

We started in the summer of 2009 with several different ideas for the company we could build. Most of the ideas revolved around the music industry and I had standing weekly calls with a dozen band managers to bounce ideas off of as we went about validating which ideas we should pursue. One of the key questions I made sure to ask was "Would this be valuable enough for you to pay for?" That screened out a lot of fun, early ideas that we would never have been able to monetize. We had tried building a consumer app the year prior and were about to shut the company down when we were accepted into Techstars. This time we swore we would build something that could generate revenue from day one, without having to get a million users first.

The managers we talked to were going around to every site where their artist had a presence and noting the number of new plays, views, fans and comments in Excel spreadsheets. They, or their assistants, would do this Monday through Friday and chart growth on a daily and weekly basis. They would skip the weekends, miss days, not collect it at the same time each day, and generally spend all their time collecting the numbers instead of actually analyzing and making sense of them.

That's when we presented them with our software that could automatically collect this data on a daily basis and allow them to export the information to Excel. They would then be able to compare this data to that of any other artist in the world and cross-reference it with concert and event data for full context. We had hundreds of conversations with managers, labels, agents and others who were trying to collect and analyze this data by hand.

In my conversations at the beginning of the summer, not one of these managers said, "Hey, you should track online data and provide a centralized dashboard to see everything going on with my artists." It was only after I showed them that we were doing that they started to say, "Wow, you would save me many hours of work each week if you could track data for my whole roster!"

It really was the first idea we struck on where potential customers were already taking time-consuming and painful measures to solve the problem on their own. We knew we were onto something when we kept hearing the same thing over and over again, from individual artists up to the biggest managers and labels in the world.

INVESTOR'S PERSPECTIVE

## NEXT BIG SOUND, by Jason Mendelson (Foundry Group)

It didn't take me long to realize that Next Big Sound was a great investment opportunity, which is somewhat ironic given that I wasn't sold on the idea at first. But I was instantly sold on the team. The pitch was as much about the people, their passion, and the problem they knew they wanted to solve, even if they didn't have the final answer. The pitch was that the founding team was, while young, broad in experience and deep in commitment to not only the industry, but to each other as partners. They were smart and self-aware.

While normally an uninteresting idea makes me think about other opportunities, I couldn't let this team off so easily. They quickly came up with their killer idea. The early pitch was simple to understand yet emotionally powerful: like baseball in the old days, the music industry is run by instinct, luck, and long-held superstitions, and that is putting it generously. The time for hard data is now, especially in light of the moneyball success in sports. Knowing that I was and am a musician, they pitched right to my emotions. As a result, I emotionally felt a connection to the problem and intellectually knew that technology had become viable to provide unprecedented insights into the industry. This became Next Big Sound.

We had invested in the music industry previously. My Foundry Group partner, Ryan McIntyre, and I had spent countless hours, and beers, discussing the future of the music industry. What Ryan and I had assumed, however, was that information was ubiquitous. After listening to the NBS team, it was clear that we had assumed wrong. What NBS pitched was that in order for any change to happen in the industry, facts, not opinions, must be known, and they would be the team to unearth, discover, digest, and provide insights around these facts. They also proved to me that most of the needed information was in the public domain, not stuck behind a paywalled proprietary database. They showed me incredible screen shots of what they would build that convinced me they could deliver a ton of information in a clear and concise manner.

They then explained in English the technical architecture, their assumptions around the costs to provide the service, and what they thought they could charge for it. One of the unique things they discussed with me was why their potential customers might hate their product. It was this discussion, which was honest, insightful and transparent, that really led me to believe they had a handle on most of the major growth issues even before they really got a start.

In the end we invested because they were doing all the "regular startup stuff": they were attacking a big market that was ready for change, had a great team, and a solid business model. Where they really stood out was their transparency, willingness to learn, and a pitch that answered just about every question that I had going into the presentation. While they hadn't built a ton of code at the time, what they built was beautiful. But the sheer amount of data they had about what they were going to do coupled with the convictions and opinions that would run the business were way ahead of most companies I see at that stage.

1. *Dragons' Den*: Season 4, Episode 3.

2. Guy Kawasaki, "The 10/20/30 Rule of Power Point," *How to Change the World*, December 30, 2005, http://blog.guykawasaki.com/2005/12/the_102030_rule.html#ixzz2uAfVcXbT

3. Alexander Osterwalder and Yves Pigneur, *Business Model Generation: A Handbook for Visionaries, Game Changers, and Challengers* (New York: Wiley, 2010).

# CHAPTER 9

# RAISING MONEY

YOUR NEED FOR CAPITAL can have a big impact on your opportunity. While we touch on fundraising briefly in this chapter, a much more comprehensive book on this topic is *Venture Deals: Be Smarter Than Your Lawyer and Venture Capitalist* by Brad and his partner Jason Mendelson.

The Timmons Model of the Entrepreneurial Process[1] lists resources as the third pillar of the startup process. While resources cover more than just capital, capital for investment is often one of the most sought after.

## THE ENTREPRENEURIAL PROCESS

The Timmons Model, Timmons, J. A., & Spinelli, S. (1999).

Recognize that many companies raise little to no outside capital. Brad's first company, Feld Technologies, only raised $10, which was used to allocate the stock between the three founders (Brad, his partner Dave Jilk, and his father Stan Feld, who was an advisor to Brad and Dave.) In many cases, you'll be able to build a successful company without any meaningful outside capital. In others, you need capital to get going and fuel your growth.

Raising capital has a secondary benefit beyond money, namely the signal it sends to the market. If you recall the discussion on signaling theory, having experienced angels or VCs invest in your company can generate a strong halo effect. Consider the halo effect that a famous entrepreneur, such as Google's Eric Schmidt, would impart to your new startup if he invested. Or how a strategic investment from Cisco Systems could validate the new collaboration software you are working on.

## BUILDING A RELATIONSHIP WITH A POTENTIAL INVESTOR

Relationships with investors are hard to develop and often take a long time. A good analogy is that you can bring the same dynamic to building your relationship with an investor to that you do when dating. When you are introduced to someone, you don't immediately ask them to marry you. Rather, you start with a first date, hopefully followed by more dates. Over time, you develop a relationship that either evolves into something beautiful or tails off and ends. Let your relationship with an investor evolve the same way.

Techstars Boulder Managing Director Nicole Glaros has a great mantra, which is that "If You Want Money, Ask for Advice."[2] Rather than approach your relationship with the investor as one where you are focused only on asking for money, take the opposite tack and ask for advice. Don't be generic about it—understand what the investor knows and has experience with, and start the relationship by approaching it with questions, rather than answers.

Explore what you can do for the investor, rather than what the investor can do for you. Fred Wilson, a VC who has an extremely popular blog, says that the best way for someone he doesn't know to get his attention is to engage with his AVC community, comment on his posts, and interact regularly through this mechanism as a way of getting to know him. Mark Suster, another popular VC blogger, talks about how he loves to invest in lines, not dots.[3] Remember, you are building a relationship. Take your time and do it the way the investor wants to do it, rather than with an aggressive, generic approach.

## WHO MAKES THE ASK?

> *Hi. My name is Bob from Buffalo. Our company, BuffaloWingz, solves the problem of hot sauce on your keyboard. We are looking for $50,000 for 5% of our company.*

Sound familiar? This is how most pitches on *Shark Tank* and *Dragons' Den* begin. But this is almost always exactly the opposite of what should happen.

When raising money for your company, the investors generally set the price. While the entrepreneur should have an opinion on the company's potential valuation, she shouldn't disclose it in the first few minutes of a discussion with a prospective investor.

Always remember that your company's valuation is negotiable. The valuation is a contractual term, negotiated by the parties involved. It is not set by formula nor is it based on a single explicit parameter, such as your company's revenue. The price an investor is willing to pay is influenced by that investor's recent funding history, the current market valuation for similar companies, and the stage of your business. Most importantly, if you have multiple investors interested in your company, you'll have more leverage on the valuation.

Investors, especially venture capitalists, often want to own enough of the company to make the investment material to them. But at the same time, investors also want to ensure that the founders maintain a large enough stake in the business to be rewarded for their entrepreneurial efforts.

## USE OF PROCEEDS

The use of proceeds is what you are going to do with the money. When discussing the use of proceeds, you should include both the actions you are going to undertake with the money, such as hiring three Bay Area-based salespeople, as well as what these actions will result in, such as generating an additional $2 million of annual recurring revenue. Once you've begun to engage with an investor, make sure you talk openly about what success means and how you are going to measure it.

Katrina Mijares pitched Toddlerobics[4] and was asked by investors why she needed to raise money. Her response was, "It will cover the market research and advertising development" in order to establish her product as a brand. This didn't please investors, who responded, "You haven't come to the table with a process to establish that brand. I hear no steps, there's no branding." Compare that to the response Trevor Bielby of Schmotoboard[5] gave those same investors, which was "to build up inventory, to put 100 of these on the floor. I have stores in Calgary willing to sell them. I plan to outsource, but with friends we can make 100 a week." Trevor was specific about why he needed to raise money while Katrina wasn't.

Like all financial forecasts based on future action, it is only important to investors that founders be reasonable, not right. No one expects you to accurately know the sales figures for new hires, but they do want to know that the cost of those new hires over a

Not all investors are created equal. Investors with valuable corporate connections, who can participate in follow on rounds, or whose participation raises other investor's confidence, are generally more valuable than investors who only bring cash to the table. Investors' reputations, especially VCs, used to be very opaque and difficult to determine. With today's world of always-connected social media, it's much easier to understand an investor's preferences and behaviors. Unless you only have one choice for an investor, do your homework on them, just like they are doing their diligence on you.

### RAISE MONEY WHEN IT'S AVAILABLE

Today some companies are raising massive funding rounds well before they need it. While this contradicts the idea above of raising the least amount of money to get to the next level, it's simply a counterbalancing dynamic as a result of market conditions. Currently the supply of early stage capital seeking great opportunities far outweighs the demand. This isn't always the case and varies dramatically by stage, sector, geography, and timing.

In general, it's relatively easy to raise early stage and late stage capital, but really hard to raise mid-stage capital. In geographies that have healthy Startup Communities,[9] there is often a vibrant early stage investor scene. This consists of experienced entrepreneurs who have cashed out of at least one business and are now reinvesting in new companies, along with early stage VCs and other wealthy individuals who are drawn to investing locally. If you start a company in a city like Boulder, raising your first $1 million is pretty straightforward.

If you have a successful business, have crossed through multiple inflection points, and are growing significantly, it'll be relatively easy for you to raise late stage capital. Institutional investors, such as late stage VCs and private equity firms, who want to invest

$20 million or more, don't care where you are located. Late stage money travels to opportunities.

The fundraise in the middle—between the first $1 million and the last $20 million—is always difficult to raise regardless of where you are in the cycle. This is the "prove it to me" zone where you have made some progress but haven't yet gotten to the point where you have an undeniably successful business.

Be opportunistic. But recognize there are cycles. It's easy today but it will be hard again, you just don't know when.

## YOU AREN'T AN EXCEPTION

When a professional investor raises a venture fund, they do so based on an investment thesis. One of the most successful funds of the last decade, Union Square Ventures, famously defined a future of valuable, new companies based on the principles of a network, summarized as "Large networks of engaged users, differentiated through user experience, and defensible through network effects."[10]

By defining what they invest in, an investor stakes out their territory. In some cases the investment thesis may even be crystallized into a set of rules, such as:

1. We will only invest in startups created under Canadian or American law.
2. We will only invest in startups in the domain of the Internet of Things.
3. We will only invest in scalable startups.
4. We will only invest in startups that have proven their model and have revenue greater than $1 million.
5. We will only invest in startups that have the potential to exit within five years.

While most VC firms publicize their investment thesis on their website, many founders fail to research and respect the goals of these investors. We see this all the time—when restaurants apply to Techstars or when professional service firms complain about the lack of capital available to them.

Don't deceive yourself by thinking you are an exception to a VC firm's strategy. Before you approach them, do some research. There is no point in asking for seed money from a late stage investor. If you are unsure of the investor's investment thesis or focus, simply investigate the last five companies they invested in to determine what these investments had in common. Spend more time researching the investors you are pitching and less time pitching investors.

Many entrepreneurs see an investment as extrinsic validation. It could be proof that the founder's crazy idea is worth pursuing, all the long hours invested by the entrepreneur were worth it, or that the road to riches is just around the corner. They couldn't be more wrong. While an investment can lead to the halo effect, receiving funding should not, in and of itself, be an endpoint. Too many founders see closing a financing round as a badge of honor, not a signal that the hard work is about to begin. Raising capital should be seen more akin to filling up your car with gas, a necessary and expensive evil. Once you've switched from bootstrapping to raising money, you have a new set of responsibilities to your investors.

Most founders think the key to fundraising is quantity of their pitches, where the more they pitch, the more likely it is that they will raise money. This is generally wrong; quality dramatically trumps quantity. Instead of investing 100 hours to make 50 pitches, the wise founder investors 100 hours to make five pitches. The majority of that time should be conducting due diligence on potential investors, understanding who will be a good fit for them, and why. There is no point in pitching a mobile telco investor on a biotech deal. Likewise, there is no point in pitching a cleantech angel on gambling software. Matching your company to the startup thesis of the potential investor is a key pre-meeting activity. Giving the same investor pitch over and over is not. Spend less time pitching and more time researching and building a foundation for the relationship.

## WHY ANYTHING OTHER THAN A YES IS A NO

Even when you have found the ideal investor and have finally gotten a meeting, this is only the beginning of the process. Remember, while this may be your only investor target, it isn't your potential investor's only choice. The demand for VC funding far exceeds the supply of smart money. The investor benchmarks are:

- For every 1,000 plans you see, you meet with less than 100.
- For every 100 companies you meet with, you will only perform due diligence on five.
- For every five companies you do diligence on, you will only invest in one.

A well-known East Coast investment fund looked at 3,000 companies last year but only invested in a dozen companies. Similarly, a well-known Bay Area investor received over 10,000 inquiries last year, yet only made ten investments. A typical Techstars program receives over 1,000 applications for ten slots. In general, the investor screening funnel looks as follows:

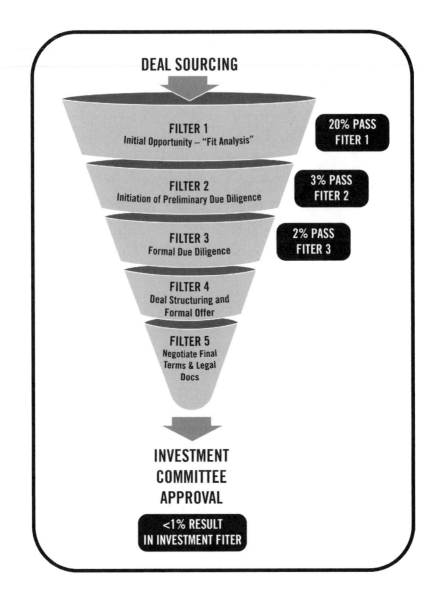

DEAL SOURCING

FILTER 1
Initial Opportunity – "Fit Analysis"

20% PASS
FITER 1

FILTER 2
Initiation of Preliminary Due Diligence

3% PASS
FITER 2

FILTER 3
Formal Due Diligence

2% PASS
FITER 3

FILTER 4
Deal Structuring and
Formal Offer

FILTER 5
Negotiate Final
Terms & Legal
Docs

INVESTMENT
COMMITTEE
APPROVAL

<1% RESULT
IN INVESTMENT FITER

As a result of this math, VCs fund less than 1% of the pitches they hear, saying no hundreds or thousands of times a year. However, entrepreneurs often don't hear the word "no." Instead they hear statements like:

- If you find a lead investor, we might be interested in joining the round
- I like it, but my partners don't
- We are interested once you have more traction

Each of the above comments is a different version of no, just said in veiled language. But even hearing this much is pleasant, since most investors fail to say anything at all. Instead they just stop responding or slow down the dialogue. There are a few reasons why many investors don't say no explicitly, including:

1. *The Option Excuse*: Investors want to leave open the option to invest later, believing that at some future date, they may wish to get in.
2. *The Missed Deal Excuse*: Investors don't want to be the firm that has to admit to passing on what became a successful company.[11]
3. *The Bad Guy Excuse*: The investor doesn't want to be the bad guy. They believe that no matter the reason they give, the entrepreneurs will say "you just don't get it" and they don't want to continue investing time in the dialogue.

Not all investors avoid saying no. Brad tries to say no to everything in under a minute.[12] He and many other VCs blog about what they are interested in and why they pass. Some investors even hold themselves to a standard of giving direct feedback to every entrepreneur they meet with.

## BE REALISTIC ABOUT YOUR VALUATION
A private company can be valued many different ways, but ultimately it is entirely subjective. While investors often evaluate a

number of key factors to decide at what price a deal makes sense to them, valuation is also about how much equity you are willing to give up and the potential returns the investment might generate.

So, how do investors decide what a company is worth? Fundamentally, they make it up, basing their view on the money invested to date, the potential returns, the risk associated with the business, the current state of the market, competition on the deal, and their decades of experience. The true value of the company is only known and set when both the investor and the entrepreneur come to an agreement on the number.

During the dot-com boom, pageviews (how many times a user goes to your website) were seen as indicators of potential value. During the Web 2.0 boom (2003–2007), the number of registered users became the metric of choice. In the aftermath of the financial crisis (2008–2009) revenue and EBITDA made a comeback.

To further complicate matters, a decade ago $5 million was necessary to get a product to market. In 2010, that number dropped to $50,000. With such a low capital requirement, many investors, especially at the early stages, have shrugged off setting valuations and instead are investing using convertible debt, which converts into equity in the next financing round, often at a discount to the price the next round investors pay.

An entrepreneur pitched the Pizza Pak,[13] a plastic pizza case that would replace cardboard boxes, to a group of investors that included international pizza magnate Jim Treliving (Chair of Boston Pizza). The entrepreneur valued his company at $1 million, yet he had not sold a single Pizza Pak. The founder claimed that his product would revolutionize the pizza industry without providing any proof of sales or customer testimonials. Even after Jim shared his expert opinion that his product would not work, the entrepreneur persisted with this idea anyway. The inflated valuation, the unsupported claims, and the blind insistence that he knew the pizza industry better than Jim Treliving only lowered his level of credibility.

## EVEN ANGELS HAVE INVESTMENT COMMITTEES

Is raising money from angels easier than from VCs? One might think that it is since angels are usually high net worth individuals who are investing their own capital. Furthermore, most VCs invest many millions of dollars per company, whereas the average angel investment is in the hundreds of thousands.

The reality, however, is not that simple. Unlike most VCs, angels are investing their own hard-earned cash, and it's often the case that investing one's own money brings a higher level of scrutiny than investing other people's money. Next, unlike VCs, the investment committee for an angel isn't made up of experienced private equity professionals meeting at a board table. Instead it is often made up of spouses meeting at the dining table. Angels typically don't have support infrastructure, such as analysts and associates, to support the transaction. Finally, many angels haven't seen dozens of term sheets, let alone negotiated them. As a result, angel investments often take as much time and energy as VC investments.

This, too, is changing. With innovations like AngelList, angel investing is being democratized and opened up to many more companies and investors.

The following investor/founder example from 3D Robotics provides a good soup-to-nuts example of taking an idea from serendipitous discovery to mere idea to MVP to full-blown product and on to a large institutional fund raising. The confluence of the right founding team with the right domain expertise and the right (read: large & nascent) market with proven demand meant that once the founder reached out to the right investor, it didn't take long for the investment to follow.

## 3D ROBOTICS, by Chris Anderson (Founder)

**Step One: Do an experiment, get mind blown**

It's 2007 and I'm editor of *Wired* magazine, with five young kids at home and a mission to bring the geek out in them (note: total failure so far). I notice that among the products that have arrived for review at the office one Friday are two boxes—one, the new Lego Mindstorms NXT robotics kit and the other a radio-control airplane. I grab them both, promising to write a review, and plan a great GeekDad weekend: make a robot on Saturday and fly a plane on Sunday.

On Saturday we dutifully build the Lego robots, which the kids promptly decide are stupid—they mostly roll slowly around and sometimes avoid walls. (They've seen Transformers—where are the frickin' lasers??) On Sunday, their main take-home lesson is that flying an RC plane is hard: it ends up in a tree, which I have to awkwardly climb, mortifying the kids and confirming their suspicions that geeky projects with Dad are always to be avoided.

In a desperate attempt to salvage what I could from the weekend, I tried to think how this could have gone better. What would have been a cooler robot and a better-flying plane? It suddenly occurred to me to simply combine the two boxes—get the Lego Mindstorms to fly the plane! I Googled "flying robot," which led me to "drone" which led me to "autopilot" which led me to a lot of math that I didn't understand and ignored.

What I did learn is that a computer, sensors, and some code (pretty much what was in the Lego box) could fly a plane. I summoned the kids for one last session around the dining room table, and a couple hours later we had what I think was the world's first Lego Autopilot. We put it in the airplane, took it to the park, and although it didn't fly well, it did at least fly. (That first Lego drone is now in the Lego Museum in Billund, Denmark.)

The kids promptly lost interest and returned to videogames, but the whole experience left me stunned. How was it possible that a dad and his kids could use Lego to build what I learned was technology regulated as a cruise missile controller? I felt that I'd suddenly glimpsed the future, much as I had when I'd tried my first Web browser 15 years earlier. Something had changed in the world that made our dining-table invention possible—but what?

**Step Two: Launch a community to see where this goes**
One thing that's always worked well for me is to ask stupid questions in public. It does two magical things: first, people answer my questions and second, it encourages other people to ask their own stupid questions. Along the way everybody gets smarter. So I set up a simple social network to do just this—understand and build on my first Lego experiment—and called it DIY Drones. It quickly hit critical mass. Lots of other people were thinking about the same things I was right then, thanks to the new availability of cheap chip-based sensors and easy-to-use hardware hacking platforms such as Arduino. Soon tens of thousands of people were starting to experiment with the new technology, much as the Homebrew Computing Club had done the same with the first cheap computer chips three decades earlier.

smartphone speed.

We had to grow even faster, so we raised another $31 million in a Series B round and started building a 21$^{st}$-century aerospace company, shooting for Google-grade software, Apple-grade hardware and Foxconn-grade manufacturing…all while still balancing the demands of an open source community with a for-profit company.

Sounds hard? It is—but it's also incredibly exciting. We feel like we're inventing the future. Today we're more than 300 employees, from our Tijuana drone factory, our San Diego engineering center, our Berkeley HQ and software team, not to mention the hundreds of open source developers around the world. This feels like the birth of a new industry, and whatever we're building it won't be anything like the aerospace companies of the past.

**Step Seven: ???**[14]

**Step Eight: Profit!**

INVESTOR'S PERSPECTIVE
### 3D ROBOTICS, by Jon Callaghan (True Ventures)

In venture capital investing, sometimes you know it when you see it.

I had known Chris Anderson for a few years when he emailed me to tell me he had a crazy idea to talk with me about. Chris and I had talked a lot about hardware over the prior few years, and he was always the most advanced thinker on the state of the sensor economy. As Chris's book *Makers* was being written, he gave me great counsel on True's investments in Fitbit, Makerbot, Tinkercad, Littlebits, and others. Chris was immersed in the robotics and hardware revolution from the beginning, so when he called me to discuss his "project that might need some funding," I cleared the decks and met him within a day or two. In my conference room in Palo Alto, Chris casually talked me through his creation of one of the most advanced commercial drone technology companies in the world.

The story was remarkable: GeekDad blog author tries to impress his kids with RC planes and starts hacking them with Lego Mindstorms...Turns to the Internet to collaborate on ideas, founds an open source movement behind DIY drones, meets co-founder over email and builds a factory. Movement takes off in all directions. A company is born.

As we talked my mind exploded with the enormous market possibilities enabled by low cost, autonomous flying vehicles. As a pilot, I immediately understood the capabilities and power that come with autopilot control, and I had witnessed how Moore's Law changed the face of commercial and general aviation in incredible ways over the past few years. As smartphones proliferated, all component costs were dropping rapidly, and the vision of a combination of robotics, low cost components and autopilot software was an easy one for me to see. As we sat in Palo Alto discussing possible applications for autonomous flight, Chris turned to me and said, "As for applications, I'm not really sure. After all, what did you need a personal computer for when they first came out?"

The investment decision in 3D Robotics was pretty straightforward in my view: Here I had one of the best thinkers and visionaries in technology that had build a company from his kitchen table to $5mm in revenues in less than two years. Not only had he done this on zero dollars, but he assembled a team and started a movement. He was building and shipping products globally, and he was at the forefront of one of the biggest potential markets of our time.

Our mission at True is to invest behind great people in great markets. It's that simple. Invest behind the smartest creative founders and work hard to be extremely early in very large potential markets. Today's creative founder is the most powerful force in our economy and society. They see the future before we do, and they push ahead to build it, fearless of the obstacles that are sure to challenge them. I believe that venture capital should be at the forefront of the solving the biggest problems of our society, pushing the bounds of the biggest and most promising technologies, and moving our understanding of science and our world forward. What we should be about is risk maximization: take the biggest risks possible in certain ways (product, market, timing), but limit risk by working with incredibly gifted founders developing core technology in a capital efficient manner.

I have made a career and built an entire firm around these beliefs, so imagine how exciting it was to meet Chris, hear his story about starting 3D Robotics, and see the future through his eyes.

True committed to lead very, very quickly.

With Chris Anderson and 3D Robotics, we knew it when we saw it.

1. Jeffrey A. Timmons and Stephen Spinelli, *New Venture Creation: Entrepreneurship for the 21ˢᵗ Century* (McGraw Hill International, 2010).
2. *Do More Faster*, Feld and Cohen (2010), p. 227–229.
3. Mark Suster, "Invest in Lines, Not Dots," *Both Sides of the Table*, November 15, 2010, http://www.bothsidesofthetable.com/2010/11/15/invest-in-lines-not-dots/
4. *Dragons' Den*: Season 4, Episode 8.
5. *Dragons' Den*: Season 4, Episode 6.
6. Douglas R. Hofstadter, *Gödel, Escher, Bach: An Eternal Golden Braid* (New York: Basic Books, 1979).
7. William J. Cameron's "Chapter 5: Find the Money to Finance Your Project" from William R. Cobb, *Business Alchemy: Turning Ideas Into Gold* (AuthorHouse, 2012).
8. Tony Bailetti and Sonia D. Bot, "An Ecosystem-Based Job-Creation Engine Fuelled by Technology Entrepreneurs," *Technology Innovation Management Review*, February 2013, http://timreview.ca/article/658
9. See Brad's book *Startup Communities: Building an Entrepreneurial Ecosystem in Your City* for a detailed discussion around startup communities.
10. Union Square Ventures Investment Thesis, https://www.usv.com/posts/investment-thesis-usv
11. http://www.bvp.com/portfolio/antiportfolio - Bessemer Venture Partners Anti-Portfolio is a refreshing counter-example.
12. Brad Feld, "Saying No In Less Than 60 Seconds," *Brad Feld blog*, June 28, 2009, http://www.feld.com/archives/2009/06/say-no-in-less-than-60-seconds.html
13. *Dragons' Den*: Season 3, Episode 1.
14. This wonderful reference comes from the South Park underpants gnomes guide to business: http://southpark.cc.com/clips/151008/underpants-gnomes

RAISING MONEY | 183

had huge amounts of sweat equity in their venture. Robert had dropped out of law school to start the business and Teresa sold the diamond out of her engagement ring. The couple borrowed money from friends and family and moved into Robert's parents' house. Investors Robert Herjavec and Lori Greiner saw, from these actions, that the couple had the determination to bring their veggie pops to market. As a result Veggie Mama was born with the $150,000 investment and a $750,000 post-money valuation.

Rest assured, no one requires you to sell your car or mortgage your home, although these are powerful signals.

### THE NO ASSHOLE RULE[3]

Creating disruptive innovation is difficult. Getting it widely adopted in the marketplace is almost impossible. Regardless of the product, service, or solution, one thing remains true—it is hard work. Innovators continuously struggle to overcome product hurdles, economic scarcity, and technological barriers. For that reason, many investors have adopted a No Asshole Rule.

Bringing innovation to the market is hard enough without having to deal with assholes. Most investors stay close to the company for a number of years, talking weekly, if not daily, to the founders they have backed. Investors want to ensure that the only source of stress comes from external forces, not internal egos.

We are not suggesting that if the entrepreneur is nice, everything will be great. Instead, we operate from the truism that "Life is too short…" The more friction an entrepreneur establishes in the early interactions with an investor, the less the investor will be interested in working with the entrepreneur.

### THE KEY PERSON DEPENDENCY

As an entrepreneur you should be collecting the best talent you possibly can, including other co-founders, investors, advisors, and early employees. Single-founder businesses are subject to a risk often referred to as a key person dependency, where the individual founder is vital not only to the innovation strategy but is also critical to the delivery process.

Kevin O'Leary is famous for asking innovators: "So what happens if you get hit by a bus tomorrow? Does the business also die?" What O'Leary is really exploring is the key person dependency issue. No one wants to fund an opportunity where the entire business is dependent on one person.

Scalability requires the innovation to be replicable. If a key person is needed to replicate the value added to the customer each time then the business's growth will be gated by the capacity of that key founder. Work hard to eliminate this dependency from the very beginning by recruiting and adding amazing people to your team.

## DRINKING YOUR OWN KOOL-AID

An echo chamber is a hollow space that produces reverberating sound. While it may be good for acoustic manipulation, it is not good for innovation. An entrepreneur who only seeks and listens to feedback that agrees with her position is said to be living in an echo chamber. Investors also refer to founders who willfully blind themselves to potential issues with their business as drinking their own Kool-Aid.[4]

An innovator who only discusses the opportunity or solution with those in the inner circle falls prey to downside of drinking his own Kool-Aid. By only listening to those who agree with you, it is likely your judgments will be biased. Many founders want to hide their innovations from the world, afraid they could be stolen. But keeping your innovation a secret and not getting critical feedback early and often is a recipe for disaster.

An essence of the Lean Startup movement is getting critical

feedback for your idea on a continual basis. That is why so many innovators in the Lean Startup movement push for sharing ideas early and often. If the only people who have told you your idea is awesome are related to you, you may have a problem.

During Season One of *Dragons' Den*, a hard-working entrepreneur was pitching a leather armchair that converted to an all-in-one exercise unit. It sounded like a horrible idea, but the entrepreneur was passionate about it. When asked why he was so enthusiastic, the founder said, "Everyone I show this to says this is a great idea. They tell me it is a great product." When the investors asked the entrepreneur who these people were, he confessed that all feedback was from close friends and family members. Without an unbiased view, especially from potential customers, this founder was demonstrating the dangers of the echo chamber.

FOUNDER'S PERSPECTIVE

## ZENIE BOTTLE, by Paul Berberian (Founder)

Memories lie.

I remember myself as a much better businessperson. In third grade, I had my first business. I sold "Genie Bottles." I got the formula from my cousin. Think snow globe, but instead of falling flakes when you shake the globe, I made a bottle filled with magic goo. When the bottle was shaken, the clear, colored liquid transformed into an opaque, iridescent storm that's as mesmerizing as a lava lamp. I made 40 bottles, took them to school and sold them for 25 cents. I sold out in minutes. (I made a cool ten dollars—without being adjusted for inflation.) Every kid at Mayfield Elementary wanted a Genie Bottle. The next day I doubled my price and doubled my production run. Kids were lining up to buy Genie Bottles before I got to school and I just knew I was going to be rich!

A struggle broke out, a bottle fell, glass broke, and kids cried. I was summoned to Sister Sheila's office and my parents were called. My Genie Bottle days were over.

Fast forward 32 years and my daughter needed to create a product to sell at her "mini-society" market, a one-day fair where kids make items and then barter to learn about commerce. My kid was going to dominate—no friendship bracelets or fuzzy pencil erasers for her. She was going to make and sell Genie Bottles. Man, she cleaned up. She sold out in 15 minutes. My wife kept one special bottle as a memento of my daughter's triumphant day of business. It sat on the kitchen window sill for three years until I needed a business idea and she handed me the bottle and said sell this.

So I did. Zenie Bottle was born because Genie Bottle couldn't be trademarked. I had come off creating a couple of successful companies and I was feeling invincible. I convinced my brother-in-law to join me as my partner and together we raised $1 million from our friends and family. Within 12 months it failed. Here is why.

We made the product more than it was. In reality it was nothing more than a cool novelty item. I felt novelties were beneath me. I was a tech CEO after all, and my ego needed a bigger idea. So I made it a photo sharing, virtual keepsake, mystery bottle with a web series backstory about the magical Zenie Bottle from the land of the Yeti. It was complex. We spent a small fortune on making all the things to support this concept and as a result the bottle became an after thought.

We were certain a market existed for the product

because I saw it go crazy twice in my life. But we never sold that product. Instead we sold the crazy idea I concocted, which turned out to be too hard to explain.

We made it out of glass but tried to sell it to kids. Moms don't like hand-blown glass bottles with a nasty fluid paired with instructions for the child to shake it violently.

We scaled the business hoping for success and made a lot of bottles, but they never sold.

I believed in my heart it would sell. I had such a strong emotional tie to the idea. Thankfully my partner did not. After we spent about $650k, we met one Saturday afternoon to discuss the business and he declared it dead. Several months of promoting resulted in only a handful of legitimate sales. I resisted but the numbers didn't lie. Only my memories deceived me. The following Monday we shut the business down.

INVESTOR'S PERSPECTIVE
## ZENIE BOTTLE, by Brad Feld (Investor)

Paul Berberian is an awesome entrepreneur. I was a seed investor in his second company, Raindance Communications, which ended up going public, surviving the crash of the Internet bubble, and ultimately being acquired by West. Paul was a classic tech/Internet entrepreneur, which is what I invest in, so when he called me and told me he wanted to talk about his new company, I was excited.

After a few minutes of listening to the Genie Bottle/ Zenie Bottle conception story, I silently thought to myself, "What the fuck is Paul doing? This is silly." But I kept listening because I had become close friends with Paul, had been successful investing in his last company, and wanted to be supportive of wherever his entrepreneurial passions took him.

At the end of the conversation, he said he was raising $1 million and asked if I'd invest. Even though I wasn't very interested in the Zenie Bottle and was skeptical that it would turn into anything, I wanted to be helpful to Paul so I invested $25,000, which was a typical angel investment for me at the time. Basically, I invested because of Paul, not because of the idea.

Over the next six months, whenever Paul and I would get together, he'd share his ever-expanding vision for the Zenie Bottle. It felt off to me, but I didn't feel like I had instincts for the business, so I was supportive, but expressed my concerns as clearly as I could.

By about nine months in, Paul had a lot of Zenie Bottles and was selling almost none of them. At this point, he started asking harder questions of himself and for the first time stopped drinking his own Kool-Aid. He knew things weren't working and was now open to feedback on whether the opportunity was actually worth spending any time on.

One day Paul called and said, "I'm done with Zenie Bottle—I'm shutting it down." We went out for a meal, had a good talk, and I gave him a big hug. He failed gracefully, selling off some of the software and recovering some money for his investors.

Several years later, I invested in the seed round of Orbotix, a new company that had gone through Techstars that Paul co-founded. Today, Orbotix is a 60+ person company with two very popular consumer products, Sphero

# DON'T QUIT YOUR DAY JOB
# IF YOU AREN'T...

### 1. PASSIONATE ABOUT THE SPACE

Being an entrepreneur is an extremely difficult job. It can be lonely, full of uncertainty, and often requires huge sacrifice. Most people need to be in love (LOVE, not like) with their startup in order to completely dedicate themselves to it. If you aren't passionate about your solution, how could your customers be?

### 2. ABLE TO EXECUTE THE SOLUTION

Ideas are nice, but execution builds value. If you aren't confident that you can not only build the solution but bring it to market, don't quit your day job (at least until you bring on a cofounder who can)

### 3. CERTAIN THAT THE PROBLEM IS A NEED (AS OPPOSED TO A WANT)

New product adoption is difficult. If your solution does not solve a compelling unmet need, it is unlikely that you'll get traction. Build solutions that are aspirin not vitamins. Find services that have inelastic demand. Don't quit your day job if your solution is only a nice to have instead of a must have.

## 4. CERTAIN THAT THE PROBLEM IS SHARED BY A LARGE (AND GROWING) MARKET

A rising tide lifts all boats. If your startup does not sell into a market that is growing year over year, and will continue to do for the foreseeable future, don't quit your day job.

## 5. ABLE TO OFFER A SOLUTION THAT IS 10x BETTER THAN ANYTHING ELSE IN THE MARKET

In order to displace incumbents, startup solutions must be exponentially better (not incrementally). If they aren't, it is unlikely that you will be able to overcome the lead and momentum market leaders have. Customers won't abandon sunk costs and accepted realities for something that is just a little better. Don't quit your day job until you have a solution that is 10x: faster, cheaper, more secure, bigger, etc.

## 6. READY TO "BURN THE SHIPS"

Explorers often burnt their ships to signal to their crew that there was no going home. Are you ready to make the same level of commitment? If not, then don't quit your day job.

## 7. ABLE TO ACCESS POTENTIAL CUSTOMERS

Today, customer-centric innovation is the focus. You need to test your product by getting it in front of actual customers. If you are limited in your ability to do, then don't quit your day job.

## 8. ABLE TO SPEND 6 MONTHS WITHOUT PERSONAL INCOME

In our always on, 24/7 global economy it takes time to develop a solution, test the market and prepare to scale. If you can't afford to wait for revenue, then don't quit your day job.

## 9. ABLE TO GARNER ENOUGH PEOPLE, USERS, AND MONEY TO CREATE A MINIMUM VIABLE PRODUCT (MVP)

Testing requires an MVP. If you can't create such (even a paper-based version) then don't quit your day job.

## 10. PREPARED TO GET INTO THE WEEDS AND DO THE GRUNT WORK

You are your startup. There are no shortcuts. Even overnight successes take lots of hard work and continuous focus. If you aren't committed to doing everything and anything needed, then don't quit your day job.

**Due Diligence**: A legal term for the process by which transactional material information is confirmed. E.g., typically before a company is acquired, due diligence will be conducted to ensure all patents are properly filed.

**Economy of Scale**: An economics concept that describes how a venture gains cost advantages from expanding sales. E.g., as the shoemaker sold more sandals, he was able to buy material in bulk. This economy of scale leads to cost savings which give the shoemaker the ability to lower his prices.

**Elasticity of Demand**: An economic theory that posits that price impacts the consumption of some products. E.g., the demand for water is inelastic since, if scarce, people will pay any price for it. The price of goldfish is elastic because demand varies with trends in pet ownership, and goldfish are not essential goods.

**Elevator Pitch**: A short verbal proposal used by an entrepreneur to illustrate the key points of an opportunity.

**Escalating Commitment**: A psychological term that denotes a decision maker's increased reinvestment of resources in a losing course of action. This bias is often caused by our desire to not accept loss. E.g., the investor wasn't prepared to write off his investment in startup X; instead he put good money after bad as part of his escalating commitment to this deal.

**Exit**: An investment term referring to a point in time when investors are able to liquidate their investment and claim their profits. E.g., when Facebook eventually goes public, the exit for many will be worth millions.

**Gating Items**: A decision-making term referring to an action that must occur before continuation. E.g., the investor made the assignment of IP a gating item to funding.

**Guerrilla Marketing**: A term for non-traditional promotional marketing that relies on time, energy and bandwidth instead of big budgets. E.g., the startup hired a chalk artist to draw graffiti on the sidewalk in front of its customers' offices as form of guerilla marketing.

**Halo Effect**: A marketing term for the goodwill one generates through positive association with a well-known brand or person. E.g., when Bill Gates joined the Board of startup XY, his halo effect led to funding as investors' confidence grew.

**Intellectual Property**: A legal term for patents, copyright and trademarks. E.g., the company had more than 100 patents as part of its strong intellectual property portfolio.

**Known and In the Know**: To be known is to have name recognition in a particular industry. To be in the know is to understand that industry and who the key players are.

**Magic Risk**: The risk associated with product development. E.g., if it is not 10x better than all other options, the magic risk will be too large.

**Management Risk**: The risk associated with leadership. E.g., having never run a startup before, the team had lots of management risk.

book is able to add at least a little to the current body of knowledge around starting companies.

Many entrepreneurs and investors contributed examples to the book. Thanks to Tim Ferriss, Isaac Saldana, Mark Solon, Carly Gloge, Stephanie Palmeri, Matt Galligan, Barbara Stegemann, W. Brett Wilson, Amanda Steinberg, Joanne Wilson, Jeff Lawson, Chris Sacca, Shane Talbott, Kevin O'Leary, Daniel Ha, Naval Ravikant, Alex White, Chris Anderson, Jon Callaghan, and Paul Berberian for their contributions.

Thanks to Steven Gedeon, Dave Valliere, and John Pinsent for their longer-form essays on complicated topics. Sean's partners and Ryerson Futures Fund also deserve some love. For all their input, for their patience, and for providing such a rich environment to learn from. Thanks to Ryerson University, Canada's home for entrepreneurship education, and its faculty for all their support.

Sean has been deeply involved in *Dragons' Den* for many years. Thanks to all the participants of the show, as well as participants of its cousin, *Shark Tank*, for baring their souls, sharing their ideas, and pitching their hearts out. Also, thanks to the Dragons, Sharks, organizers, and producers of the show(s) for bringing the art of entrepreneurial pitching and early stage funding process to prime time for so many people who had never seen it before. Sometimes funny, sometimes heartbreaking, these shows are always informative and entertaining.

Brad has learned an incredible amount from Steve Case, Scott Case, and Marc Nager through his involvement in Startup America, the Startup America Partnership, Startup Weekend, and now UP Global. Thanks, guys, for letting Brad be part of the team.

This book wouldn't exist without the help of our friends at FG Press. Dane McDonald, Eugene Wan, Kevin Kane, and Dave Heal. Your patience, diligence, hard work, and endless professionalism is inspiring.

David Cohen, the co-founder of Techstars, has contributed in so many ways, well beyond the several sidebars he wrote for this book. David, thanks for everything you do for entrepreneurs around the world and for continuing to inspire us.

Brad's partners at Foundry Group are calm listeners to all of Brad's bitching and crankiness when he's deep in the writing process. Their support for books like this, and their effort to spread joy, love, and education to entrepreneurs everywhere, is a core value that plays out daily at Foundry Group. Without them, it's likely Brad would move to Homer, Alaska and live out his days reading science fiction with his wife Amy Batchelor. Guys, thanks for everything. And, as a special bonus, thanks Jason for writing your side of the Next Big Sound example.

Finally, nothing would happen in Brad's world without the support of his wife Amy. Her endless support of his writing, her willingness to drop what she's doing and spend a day editing whatever the latest draft is, and her continuous cheerleading in the face of an onslaught of things that take Brad away from time with her is treasured.

And while on the subject of family, Sean's best investment came in marrying his wife, Marisa. During the writing of this book, somewhere between first draft and final manuscript, that investment paid a healthy dividend in the form of their son, Edison Atlas Wise. Thank you to both Marisa and Edison (the Boy Wonder) for reminding Sean what truly matters.

# ABOUT FG PRESS

FG Press is an independent publishing house in Boulder, Colorado. For more information, please visit our website at fgpress.com, or email us at info@fgpress.com.